CREATIVE
HOMEOWNER®

design ideas for
Decks & Patios

Heidi Tyline King

CREATIVE HOMEOWNER®, Upper Saddle River, New Jersey

DESIGN IDEAS FOR DECKS AND PATIOS

SENIOR EDITOR	Kathie Robitz
SENIOR GRAPHIC DESIGN COORDINATOR	Glee Barre
GRAPHIC DESIGNERS	Susan Johnston, Deborah Sottile
PHOTO EDITOR	Stan Sudol
PHOTO COORDINATOR	Robyn Poplasky
JUNIOR EDITOR	Jennifer Calvert
EDITORIAL ASSISTANT	Nora Grace
DIGITAL IMAGING SPECIALIST	Frank Dyer
INDEXER	Schroeder Indexing Services
COVER DESIGN	Glee Barre
FRONT COVER PHOTOGRAPHY	(top) Mark Lohman; (bottom right & bottom left) Liz Eddison/Garden Collection; (bottom center) Robert Stubbert
INSIDE FRONT COVER PHOTOGRAPHY	(top) Mark Lohman; (bottom) courtesy of Lloyd/Flanders, Inc.
BACK COVER PHOTOGRAPHY	(bottom left) Rob Karosis; (all others) Mark Lohman
INSIDE BACK COVER PHOTOGRAPHY	(top) Brian Vanden Brink; (bottom) Mark Lohman

CREATIVE HOMEOWNER

VICE PRESIDENT AND PUBLISHER	Timothy O. Bakke
PRODUCTION DIRECTOR	Kimberly H. Vivas
ART DIRECTOR	David Geer
MANAGING EDITOR	Fran J. Donegan

Current Printing (last digit)
10 9 8 7 6 5 4 3 2 1

Design Ideas for Decks and Patios, First Edition
Library of Congress Control Number: 2007935568
ISBN-10: 1-58011-398-2
ISBN-13: 978-1-58011-398-4
CREATIVE HOMEOWNER®
A Division of Federal Marketing Corp.
24 Park Way
Upper Saddle River, NJ 07458
www.creativehomeowner.com

Dedication

For all the do-it-yourselfers who work hard to turn
their homes—indoors and outdoors—
into comfortable living spaces.

Contents

ABOVE The right table and umbrella can set the style for your outdoor room.

BELOW Lost for decorating ideas? Take cues from the style of your house or the interior design.

RIGHT Design your new deck or patio to take advantage of a great view.

Outdoor living is here to stay—and it begins on a fabulous deck or patio. Whether you live in the Sunbelt or in a northern climate if you're like most homeowners, you're probably looking for ways to extend those easy, breezy days of summer and relaxed living in the sun and under the stars. *Design Ideas for Decks and Patios* has lots of inspiration and information to get you going.

There's lots to think about before you take on any home-improvement project—and adding a new deck or patio is no exception. You'll find out what you need to know, from site considerations to the latest

Introduction

materials—right here. Looking for ideas for a hot new outdoor kitchen? Look no further. How about creative ways to bring the comfort and sophistication of indoors to your new—or existing—deck or patio? Stylish, easy-care furnishings can do the trick, and you'll find an array of noteworthy examples on these pages, along with tips for arranging furniture for maximum comfort. There's also a host of other snazzy ideas for privacy walls, hardscaping, fireplaces and fire pits, heating devices for chilly evenings, and the latest lighting designs and water features for your consideration.

So what are you waiting for? Start living it up outdoors now.

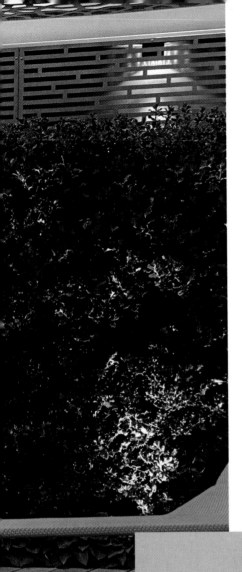

Gone are the days when a deck or patio was nice but no big deal. Today, homeowners want to brag about their "outdoor room" and all its conveniences and comforts. In fact, trends indicate that decks and patios are getting larger and feature any number of amenities. New materials and accessories make them easier to construct, maintain, and decorate, as well. The most important aspect of building a deck or patio, however, has remained constant: planning. This chapter highlights several points to consider, including choosing a site, deciding on a style, and assessing your budget.

Planning Ideas

▌ **a deck, a patio, or both?**
▌ **the site**
▌ **shapes and sizes**

What's new? A floating deck that overlooks a reflecting pool features a fushion of modern and Asian design. Note the sleek furniture and industrial materials.

ABOVE The uniformity of the square patio created from white stone tiles complements the peacefulness of the Japanese water garden.

LEFT Grass growing between the loose-set stones gives this patio an informal look.

OPPOSITE A deck provides an interesting path over a koi pond and through a perennial garden.

a deck, a patio, or both?

What better way to pamper yourself than with a fabulous getaway only steps from your living room. That's exactly what a relaxing patio or deck can do for you. These outdoor spaces may not be essential for living, but when planned properly, they can provide a relaxed, comfortable place to welcome company, hang out with family, dine alfresco, or simply unwind after a long day at work.

While decks and patios serve the same purpose, they each offer distinct features. A patio is one way to transition from the indoors to the garden. The beauty of a patio often lies in its materials, such as handsome brick, stone, or tile, and how those materials are installed. Bricks can be arranged in a variety of patterns—you may choose one that complements brickwork on your house or a pattern that adds a totally new look. Pieces of fieldstone and slate can be shaped irregularly to create random patterns or cut to work within a uniform design. You can set any of these pavers tightly or leave space between them to allow moss to grow in the openings, softening the look and adding color. Concrete, a popular material, can be uniformly shaped into any design, or it can be stamped, colored, or inlaid. Tile and interlocking pavers, which are uniform, allow you to create interesting patterns and borders.

A deck can also supply a transition from house to yard. It can be built off the ground, resolving site issues, such as overcoming a steep slope. A raised deck can improve the view as it looks over a field or beyond the treetops. As a bonus, you may be able to use the space under the deck as storage for furniture, toys, gardening tools, or pool equipment and supplies over the winter. A deck can also be multilevel—an easy way to create visual appeal in an otherwise ordinary setting—and a dramatic wraparound deck can provide access from more than one room.

1

RIGHT This long, low deck reflects the rustic appeal of the log house.

▮

BELOW LEFT A pair of separate, elevated decks provide two perfect vantage points for enjoying a rapturous view of the countryside.

▮

BELOW RIGHT The owners of this patio chose a traditional basket-weave pattern. Moss growing between the bricks adds a soft, green accent.

▮

OPPOSITE Terra-cotta tile extends the Tuscan look of the house to the floor of this "outdoor room."

||||| **versatility is a key feature of decks and patios** |||||||

a **d**eck **v**ersus a **p**atio

A patio requires flat, level ground and drainage for snow and water runoff. Otherwise, the materials (concrete or some type of paver) require little care. A deck can overcome a rough or sloping terrain because it is raised, but you must consider capacity and support. Wood decking requires regular maintenance.

Carefully consider where to locate your patio or deck and how you will use the new space. Begin by studying the traffic patterns in, around, and through the area or placement you have selected, factoring in existing or planned pathways, stairs, doors, and seating. Another consideration is the position of the sun in relation to the space. A southern exposure, which provides strong light—and heat—throughout the day, will deter moss and other plants, as well as discourage people who prefer less sunlight. An eastern exposure creates less-harsh morning sun, while a western exposure provides direct light in

the site

the late afternoon. If the site faces north, it receives no direct sunlight, which can be cooling in hot climates, but perhaps too cool in a less-temperate locale. Ground that is somewhat flat can be leveled for a patio. But if the site is sloped or the terrain is rough, a deck is the answer.

Size is another major factor to keep in mind when you are choosing a site. While you can create an inviting patio or deck of any size, make sure that it provides the space you need to enjoy it as you intended. Will it be a place to entertain? Think about adequate, comfortable seating. To cook and dine? Plan a configuration that shields diners from the heat, smoke, and fumes of cooking. To enjoy a hot tub or pool? Provide suitable privacy with shrubbery or a privacy wall.

The most obvious way to site a deck or patio is by the view. Sweeping scenery of mountains, seashore, or sky should be celebrated and enjoyed with an outdoor space that enhances the existing landscape. Positioning a patio or deck around a spectacular vista takes little thought. When the view is less than desirable or altogether lacking, transform your patio or deck into an outdoor focal point with container plantings and handsome furnishings.

ABOVE Lush plants, built-in seating and a fire pit transform an ordinary place into a special backyard getaway.

OPPOSITE A raised deck overlooks a magnificent water view here. The unobtrusive glass barrier, installed as a safety measure, is barely noticeable.

RIGHT This deck has it all: ample space, a stellar view, an imposing stone fireplace, and attractive furniture. Fade-resistant and water-repellent cushions on durable faux-wicker seating pieces are practical and inviting.

know the pros

Some do-it-yourselfers welcome the challenge of designing and installing a deck or patio. Others grimace at the thought of taking on such a project. There are professionals who specialize in this type of project. You may want to consult one.

▍**A landscape architect** must have graduated from a course in landscape architecture that includes engineering, horticulture, and architectural design. He or she can oversee the entire project, from initial design, through construction, to the installation of the surrounding landscape.

▍**A landscape designer** is not required to have formal training, but is often employed by a large nursery and is knowledge-able about design and plantings.

▍**General contractors** can manage all of the building aspects of your project. Some specialize in deck construction.

▍**Masons** lay brick and stone. In addition to installation, an experienced mason can offer you design advice regarding paving materials and patterns.

OPPOSITE Rhythm and repetition make a small backyard niche seem larger. The rectangular shape of the deck is repeated in the planters and stepping stones.

LEFT A tiered design may overcome some site problems. Crushed stone provides a soft surface for this dining area, while flagstone on the upper tier offers a platform for two butterfly chairs.

BELOW A side yard provides enough space to accommodate a small patio for outdoor dining.

▮▮ making the most of your space ▮▮▮▮▮▮▮▮▮▮▮▮▮▮▮▮▮▮▮▮▮▮▮▮▮▮▮

bright idea

layered look

Layering a variety of natural materials adds visual interest to an outdoor room.

ABOVE A circular window in the concrete wall was the inspiration for the round patio and curvy bench.

ABOVE RIGHT Wood and tile combine handsomely in this modern setting.

RIGHT A small patio overlooking a water feature is an integral part of this landscape.

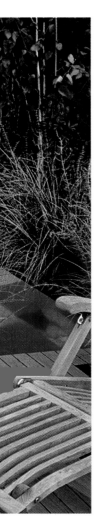

When it comes to patios and decks, it's hip to be square—and curvy, hexagonal, round, or even kidney-shape. Are you interested in multilevels, something that wraps around to the side of your house, a raised, or a ground-level design? What's right for you? Think about style and functionality. For example, do you want to reach the deck from different rooms in the house? Would you like the patio to curve around a venerable old tree? Look through magazines and books, watch television shows, and drive around, paying particular attention to yards that catch your eye. When

shapes and sizes

you have assembled a visual montage of decks and patios that you like, try to figure out why. Notice how size relates to the the size of the house. Is it the stone fireplace that draws your attention, or the built-in benches lining one side of the area? Look for recurring features and materials—examples that hint at what you are envisioning for your outdoor space.

During the design phase, incorporate your ideas into the plan, choosing one or two elements and then repeating them for impact. For example, if you plan to combine benches and a railing on your deck with an overhead structure, use common design elements. The fact that the trellis mimics the railing may not be blatant, but together they will produce a sense of harmony. Details are also important because workmanship and the choice of materials enhance the theme and strengthen the design.

The final step is to introduce a focal point. It could be a fire pit, a charming view, a water feature, or an assortment of potted plants. Accentuate your focal point with lighting and place furniture and other accessories to complement the look.

RIGHT A circular landing built around a tree is both unexpected and fun. You can incorporate important landscape features into your deck design.

▌▌▌ have it all—deck and patio combinations ▎▎▎▎▎▎▎▎▎▎▎▎▎▎

OPPOSITE TOP From this view, you can see how a deck can accommodate a number of design and lifestyle needs.

OPPOSITE BOTTOM A modest-size raised deck literally carries the inside space into the open. In this example, symmetry pulls the look together.

ABOVE A covered deck is the perfect outdoor dining room. It leads to a stone-tile patio. A solid-wood fence provides privacy in this urban setting.

LEFT Mixing wood decking material with stone tiles adds visual and textural interest to this design.

a multilevel design for more than one "room"

OPPOSITE Multilevels allow you to add more deck space in a small area and make the most of odd-shaped lots.

ABOVE Several levels, each given a specific purpose, such as dining or lounging, can break up an otherwise massive structure on a large house.

LEFT Cascading stairs and cozy landing areas that follow the slope of this steep site blend naturally into the landscape.

RIGHT Think about creating different zones or activity areas on your deck or patio even if space is limited. For example, this hot tub has been set into a small raised deck that's next to a modest patio. These two areas adjoin a screened-in room.

BELOW In the summer and during the day, this stone fireplace is a striking focal point in what the homeowners consider an outdoor family room. At night and in cooler months, it extends living time on the patio.

IIIIIIIIII a single "room" with multiple uses IIIIII

ABOVE Provide a safe way to move from one level to the next. Make sure stairs and paths are well lit at night.

RIGHT A canvas awning shades the chef on this patio's outdoor kitchen. If you plan to include a grilling spot, keep it—and the cooking heat and smoke—away from areas where guests or diners will be seated.

TOP LEFT This is an example of one deck design wraps around the house to take advantage of different views.

LEFT Details, such as the pergola, add architectural interest—and shade—to this design.

ABOVE Connected decks in different shapes and sizes enhance this lakeside property.

wraparound designs to follow the sun

dare to **b**e **d**ifferent

Think outside of the box. There are many possibilities for adding a deck. Consider an entry deck instead of the traditional front porch. Adding a master suite? Build a balcony to the front or back, or wrap it around three sides. Add a little luxury with a small deck off a bathroom, and equip it with an outdoor shower.

IIIIIIIIIIIIII creative shapes flow with the landscape IIIII

LEFT The informal, organic shape of the stone patio was meticulously planned so that the space would blend with the rustic setting and style of the house.

I

ABOVE A patio requires a level surface. This one extends from a sheltered area adjacent to the house into the open air.

I

RIGHT Small round tiles and crushed stone provide the perfect setting for this meditation garden.

During the planning stages, you would be wise to note important details about siting your new outdoor living "room." If it will be attached to your house, make sure that there is a free and easy flow between indoor and outdoor spaces, both style- and function-wise. Wherever you plan to locate the deck or patio, check whether the spot is sunny or shady. What does it overlook? Will it require wind or privacy screening? How can you improve the view and ensure your comfort whatever time of day finds you outdoors? Here are some ideas that may clear the air.

Points of View

- smooth transitions
- unattached or overlooked locations
- open-air "rooms"
- shade and privacy

Well-arranged furniture complemented by an expansive view transforms a deck into a welcoming place for conversation.

ABOVE The stark shift between the walls of the house and the seating area on the patio is camouflag[ed] by the wispy foliage of po[t] greenery and flowers.

LEFT Positioning furnitu[re] on an angle to the house keeps the patio from appe[ar]ing boxy and unimaginati[ve].

OPPOSITE A long count[er] top creates a natural tran[si]tion from the outdoor kitc[hen] to the living area without breaking visual continuity[.]

One other thing to remember is, in addition to the extra living space it offers, a patio or a deck can act as a bridge between your house and yard. For practical as well as aesthetic reasons, make the passage smooth.

If you're planning a deck, avoid long sections of stairs and use a series of landings on several levels so that the descent feels natural. Cascade levels at different points or angles rather than in one long, straight progression. Also, you may want to complement a deck by creating yet another transitional area—a patio—at ground level.

You can blend the changeover from interior to exterior living space visually using matching or complementary materials. For a patio, bricks, concrete pavers, and crushed stone are easily adaptable to your specific style, and you should be able to find ones that coordinate with similar materials on your house.

Consider shape as well, using your home's footprint as a guide. For example, plan a polygonal-shape deck that mimics the shape of the house or the roofline. Curves are attractive, but they are expensive to produce on decks. However, you might consider a curved deck or patio to

smooth transitions

coordinate with a bay or half-round window. Curved shapes can also help to integrate your deck into irregular terrain.

For continuity, don't forget to incorporate something of the interior style of your home into your outdoor room. Do it with color, furniture, and with a few decorative accessories.

RIGHT This "room" works visually because the rectilinear lines of the furniture mimic the shape of the house.
▮
BELOW Coordinate the look of both the interior and exterior rooms of your house. In this case, the furnishings share a similar style.
▮
OPPOSITE Soft furnishings and a stylish portable heater make this patio as comfortable as the indoor living room.

the principles of design work inside and out

doors and **f**olding **w**alls

▌ **Take advantage of door placement** by designing your entrance to enhance the visual flow between indoor and outdoor spaces. Better yet, install doors or folding walls so that the transition from one area to the other is not unencumbered visually as well as physically.

▌ **Go with glass doors,** if possible, so that you can enhance the feeling of one indoor-outdoor space.

▌ **A folding wall** with partitions that fold back to either side or stack separately beside each other is another option. The partitions can run the entire length of the wall and fold completely out of sight. Aluminum, wood with exterior-aluminum cladding, and all-wood folding walls are available.

bright idea

open plan

Large glass doors allow easy passage and blur the lines between indoor and outdoor spaces.

OPPOSITE Glass-door panels that slide along a top-hung track fold at hinges to provide a large opening.

BELOW Almost all-glass walls integrate the deck and the woods beyond with the indoor living areas of this modern home.

RIGHT Open archways, echoing similar ones inside the house, define a certain style on this patio.

well-designed stairs

▌**Well-built stairs** must be level, sturdy, and accessible—only then can you consider their aesthetic merits. Besides providing a decorative and utilitarian transition to the yard, they offer yet another place to add distinctive details to your outdoor space.

▌**For safety,** provide a handrail. Keep stone and wood stairs free of mold and mildew, which can become slippery. Apply rubber strips, if needed, for extra traction.

▌**Wide stairs** are easier to navigate, make a statement, and anchor the deck or patio to the ground.

▌**Stepping stones** must be flat, with as little surface variation as possible. They must be well-secured in the ground and positioned so that stepping from one to another can be accomplished with relative ease.

OPPOSITE Mixing materials adds interest. A steel frame provides support while the inlaid wood planks add warmth to these outdoor stairs.

ABOVE Angular, stacked-stone stairs create a coordinated transition from the lower courtyard to the upper patio.

LEFT Stone pavers blend handsomely with the colors of the stone planter.

ABOVE A long deck takes advantage of a harbor view.

ABOVE RIGHT A crescent-shaped landing softens the look of this urban hideaway.

RIGHT This rooftop deck has access to a master suite.

OPPOSITE Elegant furnishings create a complete outdoor room that overlooks a city.

Is there an especially lovely spot on your property where you'd like to create a quiet meditation area? A place for a hot tub, perhaps at the top of the yard, where you can watch the sun set? Or a side garden that is suitably shaded for an Old World-style patio and alfresco dinners? How about a small balcony off the bedroom or a rooftop terrace? Most of the time, you'll find that decks and patios are adjacent to the back of a house, but they don't have to be. You may be able to take advantage of a special location in your yard or a different vista with a deck or a patio that can be more than a few steps from your back door.

Adding a deck balcony can enhance the appearance of your home's exterior, particularly if you include good-looking railings or an attractive privacy wall. It can be the roof of your garage or that of a city apartment. However, before you start planning, check with your local building department to find out what is allowable or required. Communally owned buildings usually have very specific policies about rooftop terraces and decks.

unattached or overlooked locations

Of particular concern is whether your roof can support this type of use. Decking material is relatively lightweight. But you will have to leave space between the decking and the roof's surface for drainage. It's also easy to remove if you have to make roof repair, unlike paving. Although interlocking pavers are not difficult to remove, they are considerably heavier than wood.

bright idea

details

For interest, mix railing
materials. Or match
railings with other
architectural features
of your house.

creative railings and walls define your space | | | | | | | | | | | | | | | | |

OPPOSITE A stacked-stone wall defines this patio and visually separates it from the gently sloping lawn.

ABOVE Modern in their appeal, steel cables look interesting mixed with wooden posts and keep the view unobstructed.

LEFT Stone walls and iron fencing provide a secure enclosure for this terrace balcony.

borders

▌**If you want your outdoor space** to have the intimacy of an indoor room, a border is essential. Hardscaping with walls and fences is the most common way to define an outdoor area, but you can also use a natural shrubbery border or potted plants.

▌**Borders can also be functional.** For safety, add a small knee wall when the ground beyond your patio slopes downward. When privacy is an issue, incorporate a fence or trellis into your design. A wall or railings around a deck are the ideal place for installing built-in seating.

ABOVE This boxy planter contrasts with the curvy wall, introducing a new shape for visual variety.

ABOVE RIGHT The fire pit is part of a large stone patio.

RIGHT A naturalistic rock wall with a waterfall looks and sounds refreshing on this stone patio.

Open-air rooms can be as practical and livable as their indoor counterparts, and they are often more romantic and charming. However, there is one unpredictable element that affects all aspects of a room outside—the weather. Taking time to plan for this uncontrollable element will make all the difference regarding how much time you spend there.

open-air "rooms"

If you have long winters, extend your time outdoors by installing heat lamps or portable heating units, strategically positioning them near seating and dining areas. Consider a fire pit or outdoor fireplace for additional warmth. Surround your patio with a knee wall or secure your deck to an exterior wall as a deterrent against wind.

In hot climates and during summer, add awnings, umbrellas, or some other kind of shade covering. Sturdy trellises covered in ivy or other vines will also provide relief from overhead sun, as well as a sound structure for attaching an all-weather ceiling fan. Add lots of shrubbery and foliage to absorb the heat, too. Fountains can enhance a cooling effect as well as adding the delightful sound of moving water. In extreme climates, consider a residential mister that will periodically spray a cool mist of water into the air.

Retractable awnings can be extended when needed, or you can simply build a roof over your patio or deck for year-round protection. This can be as elaborate as tying the structure into your home's existing roofing system or as straightforward as constructing a freestanding pavilion on posts secured in the ground.

LEFT An outdoor fireplace is both a focal point and a source of warmth on cool nights. It extends the outdoor season past the summer.

ABOVE Terra-cotta tiles absorb heat rather than reflect it in this year-round mild climate.

RIGHT Look for all-weather furniture and fade-resistant upholstery that can withstand extreme heat and cold.

separate but **e**qual

Some activities need their own dedicated space. For example, you may not want to sunbathe next to the grilling station. Or you may not want the kids' play area to intrude upon an adults' entertainment space. Some solutions might include:

▍**A multilevel design** to accommodate different needs.

▍**Dividing the space** with built-in or freestanding planters, a trellis, privacy screens, or outdoor curtains.

▍**Separate** "rooms" in different areas in your yard. (See page 41.)

ABOVE LEFT An English garden becomes a stunning backdrop for an intimate morning breakfast on the deck in the early morning sun.

ABOVE Late afternoons are cool and shady in this spot, making it ideal for lounging before dinner.

LEFT Comfortable chairs are positioned in front of the fire on cool days and fall evenings.

when the sun comes out

▌ **How much sun** and shade you want is an important consideration when positioning your deck or patio. A deck on the north side of your house will receive no direct sunlight. This may be the best exposure in a hot climate.

▌ **An eastern exposure** provides morning sun and afternoon shade. This is often the best exposure for warm climates.

▌ **In cold climates** a southwestern exposure provides full late-afternoon sun, creating warmth after lunch on cool days in the spring and fall.

▌ **The sun's angle** is also important. The sun is highest in summer and lowest in winter. That means a south-facing deck or patio will be its hottest in summer.

ABOVE A sturdy roof protects this outdoor kitchen and patio from sun and rain.

▌

RIGHT A patio with a southwest exposure is perfect for alfresco dining in the early evening.

bright idea

hung over

Extending an overhang protects the patio from the elements without blocking sunlight. Lush landscaping creates outdoor "walls."

ABOVE A fabric canopy provides shade for this outdoor kitchen and dining area.

OPPOSITE LEFT These trees offer a natural filter for harsh sunlight.

OPPOSITE RIGHT Dense landscaping and a thatched roof transform a small patio into a tropical enclave.

shade and privacy

Too much sun can limit the amount of time you spend outdoors. For instant shade, add awnings, extend the overhang of your house, or construct a trellis topped with fabric or vines that cover the openings to block the sun.

Privacy is an equally important issue. While the appeal of a deck or patio is the location—outdoors—there can also be drawbacks. Your first decision is whether you want an airy, open room or one that is cozy and secluded. A small space will feel cozier—or less crowded—than a large deck. Low benches and railings with large open sections can give you seclusion without making you feel crowded. In addition, a long, narrow deck or patio that hugs the house will be more private than one that juts into the yard.

If the deck is high, you may be visible to passersby. That problem can be solved with a partial wall, a trellis, outdoor curtains and shades, or a canopy tent. Screening can also provide some privacy.

bright idea

natural beauty

Keep furnishings and details simple when your deck or patio is surrounded by a great view.

ABOVE The deck and furniture are crafted from the same type of wood, which unifies the overall look here.

RIGHT A pair of comfortable chairs is all that's needed for this rooftop deck.

the outdoors is great when the livin' is easy

Aesthetics, maintenance, and durability are important factors that determine what type of material to use when building a deck. Fortunately, today you have options. In addition to traditional wood decking, there's pressure-treated lumber, man-made composites, and vinyl decking. A variety of blind fastening systems offer a cleaner look for deck surfaces, too, while under-deck drainage systems help to eliminate dampness that can destroy wood. To assist you in deciding what material will best suit your lifestyle and budget, this chapter presents the pros and cons of each one.

Deck Materials

- natural wood
- pressure-treated wood
- composites
- finishes

Wood decks require a water-repellent finish to keep the wood from shrinking and splintering.

Nothing beats the beauty of natural wood. When constructing a deck, three types are commonly used: redwood, cedar, and cypress. *Redwood* has long been a favorite because of its handsome straight grain and ability to absorb finishes well. Heartwood redwood is also resistant to rot, decay, and insects—the most common enemies of outdoor wood

natural wood

structures. Its only drawback is price. In some parts of the country, the cost can be four times as much as pressure-treated wood. (See page 62.) However, you can save money by using redwood for parts of the deck you will see and relying on pressure-treated wood for structural components. Ranging in color from light to dark red, redwood can be stained or left unfinished to weather to an attractive silver hue.

Cedar decking, most typically western red cedar, has many of the same qualities as redwood but costs significantly less. Heartwood cedar is rot- and insect-resistant and easy to work. Softer than redwood, cedar should be a No. 1 grade for structural components. The custom clear grade is appropriate for a clean, contemporary look, while the knotty grade has a rustic quality. Cedar can be left untreated so that it weathers to a pleasing gray, but it also takes finishes better than some other woods.

Bald *cypress* is well-known throughout the American Southeast, where the trees thrive in swampy marsh areas. This wood is naturally resistant to rot and insects. While cypress does not readily absorb water, it takes a long time to dry once moisture is absorbed and therefore must be dried carefully before use to prevent twisting and warping. In the Southeast, cypress can be affordable, but it increases in price the farther it has to be shipped away from its habitat. Colors range from tan to red, with a weathered look of gray.

OPPOSITE Choose decking material that suits your taste, your lifestyle, and your budget.

BELOW A redwood deck will cost more than most other types, but it will hold up well against moisture, insects, and decay.

bright idea

grades

Choose one of the heartwood grades for a deck or parts of a deck that will be on or near the ground. Use a sapwood grade if insects or decay won't likely pose a problem.

bright idea

looks cost

Save money by reserving costly exotic woods for what's visible—the decking and rails. Use fir or pine for the unseen structural supports.

ABOVE In addition to its longevity and durability, wood is prized for the handsome variations in its warm tones.

RIGHT Weathered to a matte gray, this Cambara mahogany deck shows no signs of checking, cupping, or splintering.

OPPOSITE Twice as strong as oak and more durable than redwood, Brazilian Ipe is a high-quality hardwood.

exotic woods: pros and cons

Extraordinarily dense and rich with natural oils, exotic woods such as Ipe (Pau Lope, ironwood, or Brazilian walnut), teak, Brazilian cherry, or Philippine mahogany live up to their promise of being strong, maintenance free, and long lasting. These characteristics make them resistant to decay, fungal growth, wood-boring insects, and even fire.

The downside to using an exotic wood or decking is that, because it is so solid, it generally requires predrilling and pilot holes prior to driving the recommended stainless-steel fasteners. In addition to the extra labor charges that work will incur, exotics cost as much as redwood. To retain their color, they will require regular maintenance.

most hardwood decks require minimal maintenance

For most homeowners, pressure-treated (PT) lumber is the most cost-effective, accessible, and practical material for building decks. Pine, hemlock, and fir are the most common types of wood, and once treated, they are all extremely resistant to rot and insect damage. Although pressure-treated lumber is hard, it can be drilled or nailed fairly easily. You probably won't have to predrill any holes before the installation.

pressure-treated wood

How does lumber become pressure treated? The process involves placing the wood in a vacuum chamber that is filled with liquid preservative. Varying degrees of penetration determine how the lumber is graded. As an example, wood that is rated for aboveground use contains less preservative than wood that is rated for ground contact, for obvious reasons.

In the past, arsenic was used to treat the wood, but concerns about leaching from lumber used for home decks, playgrounds, and other applications prompted investigation by the Environmental Protection Agency. As a result, the lumber is now treated with copper compounds that are more friendly to the environment and pose no known threat to humans (but may affect marine life). These compounds, however, are highly corrosive. Therefore, hot-dipped galvanized and stainless-steel nails and screws are recommended for fasteners.

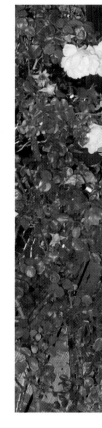

The colors of pressure-treated wood range from dark greenish-brown to a light brown. When it's left unfinished, the wood weathers to light tan or gray. If you want to paint or stain it, let the wood cure, or dry, for at least six months before applying the finish. Because of the changes in the treatment process, today's pressure-treated wood costs about 10 percent more than in the past.

ABOVE Left unfinished, pressure-treated lumber weathers to a mottled brown. The wood will also shrink slightly in width after installation.

BELOW Here is another example of pressure-treated wood's versatility.

RIGHT Different preservative levels are available, including one for wood that will be in contact with the ground.

how to **c**are for **y**our **d**eck

Even the most maintenance-free decks require some upkeep. Routine care, such as removing twigs and leaves from the surface of the deck, will deter more serious problems from developing.

Sweep and pressure-wash your deck frequently. Remove dirt and other debris from the joints, and wash away patches of mold and mildew. Take care not to apply so much pressure that the stain or paint finish is damaged. Some people also pressure-wash their decks with a solution of bleach and water, but water by itself is generally strong enough to clean the surface.

Apply a high-quality sealer to protect wood from moisture, mold, mildew, rot, and fading. Sealers contain water repellents and UV inhibitors, which protect against the harmful rays of the sun. You can also add a fungicide, mildewcide, and insecticide to paint or stain when you purchase it. Resin, or "alkyd resin," also repels water by soaking into the wood and sealing it from moisture without hardening on the surface. A heavy application will give your deck a slight sheen.

▌▐ finishes and stains can enhance wood's good looks ▐ ▌▐ ▌▐ ▌

ABOVE LEFT Although a roof protects the wood floor of a gazebo from the elements, a high-gloss varnish was applied for both its visual appeal and to further limit deterioration from debris and rain.

▌

ABOVE Sealers with resin cover a deck with a lustrous sheen.

▌

LEFT Shaded decks are especially susceptible to natural debris. Pressure wash it as needed to remove mold and mildew.

Once used only in commercial projects, composite, or man-made, materials have become quite popular with homeowners. No doubt the reason is that synthetic products are virtually maintenance free. There are several types of synthetic materials available, and it is prudent to take time and learn about the aspects of each. Some products are made from wood fiber and plastic reclaimed from wood waste and recycled plastics. Others are made from

composite materials

vinyl. Both are primarily used for decking, but many manufacturers also offer matching components for guardrails and handrails.

There are several advantages to synthetic decking products. They are not susceptible to rotting and checking, and they don't splinter—a real benefit if you have young children who will be on hands and knees on your deck. The boards come precolored so you don't have the extra task and cost of finishing once your deck is built. Some types are easy to bend, creating opportunities for interesting railing and decking designs that you

ABOVE The flexibility of synthetic wood products offers a variety of creative opportunities, including the inlay and curved benches shown here.

RIGHT Although synthetic decking will eventually weather, the process takes much longer than with its natural counterparts.

don't normally have with wood. And because synthetic wood requires less maintenance, you'll have more time to enjoy your deck.

The biggest drawback to a composite product is its price—often much higher than that of a top-quality wood product. You can recoup some of the cost because the product isn't labor intensive, but you will still pay more for it.

There are other cautions about composite materials. Dense types of synthetic lumber hold more heat than real wood, which can cause discomfort when you're walking on them with bare feet. Also, some brands are heavy and dense, making them more difficult with which to work than wood. And as much as manufacturers try to make composites look like the real thing, many don't.

bright idea

a green deck

For wood, find sources certified by the Forest Stewardship Council and the Sustainable Forestry Initiative. For synthetics, check out the Healthy Building Network for environmentally preferable materials.

ABOVE LEFT Aluminum planks have a high-gloss shine. Purchase railings to match your decking.

OPPOSITE BOTTOM Aluminum is a good choice for decking when you want to mix and match materials. Here, wood railings complement the aluminum decking.

ABOVE Some synthetic materials are considered environmentally friendly because they are made of recyclable materials.

the **a**luminum **a**lternative

An aluminum deck? You'd be surprised how attractive this type of decking material can be. Among its benefits is less maintenance. Plus, it's lightweight but strong. Aluminum decking is made from recyclable materials and it has a clean, contemporary look. The material is substantial, so denting and noise are not issues. Finally, it installs much faster than wood decking.

So how does it work? Aluminum planks interlock to form a waterproof surface. Built-in channels between the planks carry away rain, so no additional under-deck drainage system is needed. There are several colors from which to choose. For installation, you won't need special tools, either.

finishes

The structural soundness of your deck depends on the building materials you choose. Its finish, however, can also contribute to your deck's longevity. Rain, ice, snow, abrasion from traffic, and constant sunlight all work to wear down your deck's durability. To make matters worse, the joints between the many parts of a deck retain moisture long after the rain stops, making the wood vulnerable to rot, mildew, and insects. The good news is that manufacturers have developed a variety of sealers, preservatives, UV-light inhibitors, pigments, and resins to combat this barrage.

Clear sealers, or water-repellent preservatives, are the most popular choice for new decks, helping prevent wood from cracking, warping, cupping, splintering, and checking. Sealers are clear, but sealed wood will continue to weather to gray.

Toners, or transparent stains, offer more protection than clear sealers. They enhance the color of the wood but allow the grain to remain visible. When used on pressure-treated lumber, the look will resemble that of more-expensive woods. The best products in this category penetrate the wood surface, protect it from UV light and mildew, and leave a substantial top layer to prevent moisture absorption. *Semitransparent stains* have more pigment and work well to hide imperfections in the wood. Alkyd, or oil-based-versions excel because they penetrate wood better than acrylic formulations.

Solid-color stains resemble thinned paint. They protect against UV rays and hide the color and grain of the wood. Oil-based products last longest, but water-based formulas are easier to clean up.

Deck and porch paints are film-forming products. This makes for superior UV and moisture protection and is ideal for camouflaging lesser grades of lumber. Paint, however, can blister and peel, and will eventually show wear in high-traffic areas.

Preservatives are not paint but additives with specific properties, such as preventing fungal growth, rot, and decay. Preservatives can be applied before painting or added directly into paint or stain.

RIGHT Distinct areas have been created by using two different finishes. The weathered seating area blends nicely with the stone fireplace, while the area in front of the fireplace features a rust-colored floor.

OPPOSITE TOP Painted rails and stairs reflect the light color of the sand. Copper details add a decorative touch.

OPPOSITE BOTTOM Opaque marine paint protects the wood surrounding an outdoor spa.

apply a preservative to untreated wood to prevent decay

RIGHT A natural stain protects the wood but allows the grain and knots to show.

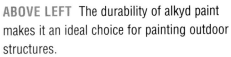

ABOVE LEFT The durability of alkyd paint makes it an ideal choice for painting outdoor structures.

ABOVE Deck stains and paints can be custom mixed to match the color of your house.

4

L ocal building codes, the climate, and the slope of your yard are factors that can influence your decision about whether to build a patio rather than a deck. Another one is aesthetics. Depending on its shape, a patio can blend almost organically into the landscape. However, one other important consideration is your budget. A patio is usually more costly to install than a deck, but the materials—tile, brick, stone, and concrete—are durable and require little maintenance if there is proper drainage. They can be arranged, combined, and in the case of concrete, colored or textured to create a one-of-a-kind look.

Patio Paving Material

▮ materials and installation

Blue slate is a classic choice for a patio. The random sizes of the stones used here and their irregular edges add interest to the surface.

As you think about material for your patio, consider what will work best with your home's style.

Classic and extremely durable, *brick* is available in a variety of colors, surface textures, shapes, and thicknesses. Common brick and half-thickness paver bricks can be fashioned into patterns and set in sand or applied on top of wet

materials and installation

mortar. A dry-laid installation combines sand and cement, which is dampened after the mixture has been poured between the bricks. As it dries, the mortar hardens.

Stone is a natural choice for patios. Like brick, you can choose colors, textures, shapes, and thicknesses, and it can be installed directly into the soil or by setting it in sand or wet or dry mortar. Although stone can be laid out uniformly like brick, many homeowners prefer a free-form pattern dictated by the individual shapes of the stones. Granite, limestone, slate, bluestone, and sandstone are the most common types.

Poured concrete is one of the least-expensive options for patios, and one of the most versatile. You can score it to resemble tile, or stamp or trowel it to create designs and textures. You can also paint or stain concrete, or inlay it with small bits of things such as pebbles, shells, or broken tiles.

Concrete pavers and tile are also popular. *Pavers* are available in numerous shapes, sizes, and colors and are less expensive and easier to install than brick. *Tile* can be costly, but its beauty is unmatched. Terra-cotta, synthetic stone, and quarry tile each present an array of options, and all are applied on top of wet mortar. Tile is more prone than other materials to crack, so make sure it can endure weather conditions in your area.

RIGHT Earthy and warm, unglazed terra-cotta tile is an excellent choice in a temperate climate.

OPPOSITE Brick pavers are at home anywhere. This basket-weave pattern has a formal look.

interlocking pavers

Interlocking pavers do exactly as their name implies: they lock together to prevent lateral movement, which keeps them intact under heavy weight or in extreme climates. If they are set in sand, the space between them will allow for drainage and expansion. Pavers can also be mortared in place.

When uniform pavers are used, they create a traditional cobblestone effect that is ideal for garden settings, formal entertaining areas, and walkways. Turf blocks, a variation of pavers, are laid to form a solid, flat surface and protect the ground from traffic. Their waffle-weave pattern allows ground covering to grow between the blocks.

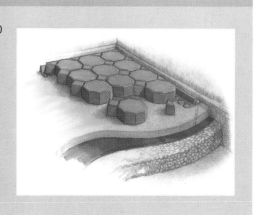

dry-laid designs in stone or brick are less formal

OPPOSITE Irregular pieces of stone set into concrete blend handsomely with this Spanish-style stucco house.

LEFT Interlocking concrete pavers provided an easy way to create a small patio in front of this pretty garden shed.

bright idea

motifs

Patterns may reinforce a design theme. Left, the circle around the landing reflects the curves created by the cascading retaining walls.

LEFT Gray mortar contrasts with the rustic red of this patio's terra-cotta tile. The effect emphasizes their shape and creates a striking honeycomb pattern.

OPPOSITE BOTTOM Brick can be set into a number of interesting patterns on patios and in borders.

RIGHT Stone can be a cool surface underfoot. Here, random shapes add interest to a small patio.

wet-**m**ortar **i**nstallation

A wet-mortar installation for brick, tile, and stone has several benefits. As it dries, the mortar hardens, holding the pattern in place and making an extremely durable surface.

Installation methods for a wet-mortar application vary, but the most common involves framing and pouring a slab, then laying materials directly on top. Some homeowners may feel confident about tackling small wet-mortar projects, but hiring an expert ensures that the site is level, the mortar mixture is correct, and the surface material is secure.

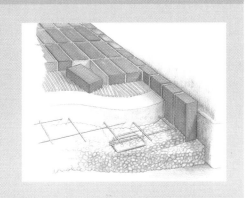

the **v**ersatility of **c**oncrete

A number of techniques can be applied to dress up the surface of an ordinary concrete slab, and they are usually less expensive than the cost of installing tile, brick, stone, or pavers.

The pros. Concrete conforms to almost any shape and space. It can be colored, scored, textured, and embellished to create a unique patio surface. And because concrete provides the foundation for other materials, you can cover it up when you get tired of it.

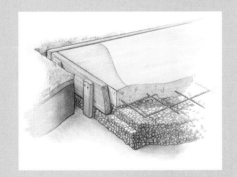

The cons. In extreme weather conditions, concrete contracts and expands, forming cracks. You must include expansion joints in your design. If finished with a smooth surface, concrete can be slick. Because the mixture dries fast, concrete installation is best left to the professionals.

OPPOSITE The scored concrete on this French Country-style terrace has the look of large stone tiles.

ABOVE Polished concrete has a smooth surface and light sheen. Grass "grout" accents and softens the look.

LEFT The color variations in Mexican saltillo tile add to its rustic charm.

ABOVE Blue 4 x 4-in. slate tiles add color and pattern to this shaded retreat.

OPPOSITE Large ceramic tiles define this patio's sitting area.

tile style

▌**Ceramic tile** comes in many colors, shapes, and sizes, and it is easy to clean, making it an exceptional material for patios. However, tile can crack when it is exposed to harsh temperatures. For the most part, ceramic (and clay) tile is best reserved for temperate climates.

▌**Glazed** ceramic tile has a shiny finish that repels water, making it slippery when wet. It is best used outside as accent tiles or on vertical surfaces.

▌**Unglazed** ceramic tile absorbs water and is safer to walk across, so it is usually recommended for exterior projects. Standard sizes for ceramic tile range from 4- to 20-inch squares.

ABOVE A small, circular breakfast terrace complements the rounded stairs leading into the garden.

OPPOSITE An awning and curtain panels that open and close provide shade and privacy in a stylish manner.

a terraced patio has charm

5

A deck or patio can be equipped for a variety of uses, from sunbathing and reading to entertaining and cooking. So the space has to be comfortable, or it's doubtful that you'll spend enough time there to appreciate your investment. Consider protection from the elements of wind, sun, and rain—and pesky insects. Hardscaping with structures such as gazebos, arbors, and trellises can also provide handsome ways not only to define your space, but to add privacy, deflect noise, and shelter you and your furnishings from the hot rays of the sun. Here are some ideas for your project.

For Your Comfort

▌ partial or complete shade?
▌ gazebos, arbors, and trellises

Comfortable outdoor spaces are both functional and inviting. This sunny deck requires shading for part of the day, and an umbrella seems to do the trick.

Enclosures for your deck and patio can serve a number of purposes, often providing shade, privacy, and drama all at one time. Wind screens are specifically designed to deter strong breezes with solid barrier walls or by redirecting air through slats that act as filters. Pergolas, which have aesthetic appeal, deflect wind as well as create shade. For

partial or complete shade?

mosquitoes and other insects, traditional screen enclosures continue to be your best defense. For do-it-yourselfers, screening is available in a variety of colors, and because frames are usually easy to construct, they offer flexibility for choosing how much of your deck or patio you want to enclose.

When shade is desired, consider an easy-to-install umbrella. It can add color and pattern to an outdoor dining table or seating area, but it also provides much-needed cover in a specific area. An 8- or 12-foot umbrella is large enough for ample coverage yet easy to open and close. For stability, opt for a heavy base or choose an umbrella stand that can be bolted in place.

TOP A pergola filters light without blocking it. For extra cover or to cool a hot spot with shade, plant a vine.

BOTTOM A fabric umbrella, treated for outdoor use, is an easy way to pull together your decor—and it creates a place out of the sun for entertaining or dining.

OPPOSITE An antique wrought-iron arbor adds a bit of Victorian charm to this outdoor seating area.

umbrella **s**hopping

A well-made umbrella will have a sturdy post, well-secured ribs, and heavy-duty material, such as acrylic canvas or PVC fabric. The most expensive types will also feature a tilting mechanism that allows the angle of the umbrella to be altered to block the sun from any direction. No-post umbrellas can be suspended from an overhead structure.

OPPOSITE TOP Coordinating the umbrella with chair cushions brings continuity to a design. Here, strands of small lights have been wrapped around the umbrella's ribs to set the mood for a party.

OPPOSITE BOTTOM This umbrella's wood pole and ribs feature a teak finish that looks elegant paired with leather high-back chairs and a metal table.

ABOVE A tiki or thatched umbrella may be created from natural fibers, such as palm or willow, or it can be a man-made look-alike. Mexican barrel chairs enhance the decor.

freestanding umbrellas allow flexibility

OPPOSITE This free-standing umbrella has a large adjustable clamp that can be mounted to most deck rails.

RIGHT An Asian-inspired design, this umbrella comes with a bamboo post. The vivid color coordinates beautifully with the brick patio and the chairs.

BELOW Place an umbrella behind a chair to create a comfortable reading spot out of the sun's glare.

bright idea

weight to go

A typical market umbrella needs a 70-lb. stand to keep it from tipping over on a breezy day.

ABOVE This wooden garden pavilion has side and corner curtains that can be easily drawn for shade and privacy or tied back to permit air and cooling breezes inside.

ABOVE RIGHT An outdoor daybed with a canopy brings a touch of Bali to a rooftop patio.

RIGHT The heavy canvas awning and matching royal-blue cushions add a tropical touch to this garden spot.

OPPOSITE Loose gathers of sun-shade fabric are soft and billowy, giving this outdoor room a casual, comfortable vibe.

shade sails and awnings

▌**Shade sails** are so named because they provide shade with "sails." They are stretched tautly across an area or woven in billows between the frame of a pergola.

▌**Fabric awnings** attach to your house or a structure and can be manually or electrically retracted as needed. Both shade sails and awnings are made from heavy canvas or PVC.

IIIIIIIIIIIIIII **a pergola adds structural detail to a design** II

OPPOSITE Romance the look. Hang a candelabra from a hook that's attached to the pergola.

ABOVE A small, overhanging slatted shelter offers just enough protection and adds charm to this cottage patio.

RIGHT TOP This design for a log-house deck has rustic appeal.

RIGHT MIDDLE Massive columns and strong beams look imposing over the stone walkway leading to a patio.

RIGHT BOTTOM If your budget is tight, use less-expensive wood and paint it your favorite color.

OPPOSITE A lush vine emphasizes the elegance of arched French doors that lead onto a small patio.

ABOVE A canopy of vines entwined around a pergola provides some shade over the dining table on this sunny deck.

RIGHT Create a natural privacy screen by surrounding the area with lots of plantings.

the **r**ight **v**ine

There are many vines from which to choose, but it is best to consult with a professional before making your decision. Factors to consider include whether the vine flowers, is slow- or fast-growing, needs sunlight or shade, has thorns or messy foliage, requires much maintenance, and is temperamental.

bright idea

climbing vines

Climbing vines fill in open spaces of a pergola or trellis, in turn providing privacy and protection. They can climb up and around a structure, and they make lovely focal points.

walls and **s**tructures for **p**rivacy

Privacy, a major factor when planning an outdoor room, is easy to accommodate when considering other structures that are essential or desired. Retaining walls, screens to block wind and sunlight, and open air pavilions with freestanding walls all serve a specific purpose while also adding privacy and intimacy to your space.

LEFT A solid wall was the only way to create privacy in this small outdoor area, but the pergola and lattice allow air and light to filter into the space.

ABOVE A stone retaining wall shores up the hill behind but also serves as a wind shield for the dining area.

RIGHT Lattice walls provide some screening without totally blocking the view of the lake.

BELOW A tall fence acts as a solid wall on one side of this pavilion, but the feel of the space is open and airy.

ABOVE A rustic vine-covered slatted roof offers natural shade to this patio.

RIGHT Elegant fluted columns support an architecturally interesting ceiling composed of beams and lattice.

OPPOSITE TOP A partial roof protects one section of this patio while a pergola offers some shelter to the area that extends beyond the house. Painting both structures white provides visual continuity.

LEFT Angled horizontal slats on the surrounding screen contribute to the orderly layout and look of this well-structured garden.

RIGHT Slats fastened at an angle on posts provide a shuttered appearance.

OPPOSITE BOTTOM LEFT Privacy and ventilation are at a premium with angled wood slats.

OPPOSITE BOTTOM RIGHT Natural materials blend organically with the landscape.

angled slats allow ventilation and privacy

ABOVE Ornate spiral, or roped, columns support heavy wood beams that help to form a sheltered pavilion on this Mediterranean-inspired terrace.

OPPOSITE LEFT The deck's understated and simple gazebo has a wooden-shake roof that's appropriately casual for its beach setting.

OPPOSITE RIGHT A pretty white-painted gazebo looks charming sitting at one end of a country-garden patio.

A trellis, arbor, or gazebo provides an opportunity to add style, as well as some type of shelter, to your deck or patio. It's best to incorporate these elements during the planning stages of your project, but if the budget is tight, you can add them later.

Be mindful, however, that if you plan to add a large gazebo or an arbor to your deck, you'll have to provide extra footings and support for the additional weight. (That's a good reason to include these structures with your original plan.) If you are adding one of these structures to an existing deck, look at your home's architecture for style inspiration. Soffit brackets, cornice molding, and fascia widths all offer design cues

gazebos, arbors, and trellises

that you can use to bring continuity to your project. Try to mimic roof angles and configurations, and if possible, match or complement your home's color scheme so that the new outdoor structure coordinates with the rest of the exterior.

LEFT This deck design strikes the right balance between an open space and shelter.

BELOW LEFT A fountain wall provides a focal point for this dining area.

OPPOSITE This open structure defines space without closing it off from the garden.

focal points

Like interior spaces, outdoor rooms need a focal point. Almost any structure that contrasts with its environment can become a focal point, but the key is to choose something that also relates to its surroundings. Architectural salvage—garden gates and window frames—fountains, walls, structures, and garden art are all effective at garnering attention.

6

The Europeans have known for centuries that outdoor rooms can be just as functional and comfortable as their indoor counterparts. After all, what could be more enjoyable than dining with good friends and family underneath a shady canopy of trees or a blanket of twinkling stars? To transform your new deck or patio into an inviting spot for entertaining, start with something as simple as comfortable outdoor furniture or spring for a top-of-the-line outdoor kitchen. This chapter offers pages of ideas to inspire you along with good advice to help you make your plans happen.

Entertaining Ideas

- outdoor kitchens
- fireplaces and fire pits
- pools and spas
- media
- dining in style

New weather-resistant materials and fabrics let you furnish your outdoor living space as comfortably as any room that is inside your home.

All you need to cook outdoors is a grill, but to truly create an outdoor kitchen, the same considerations given to the planning of an indoor room should be applied. The first is to pinpoint exactly how you want to use the space. Are you primarily interested in grilling, or do you want the ability and space to

outdoor kitchens

prepare an entire meal? Do you need an adjacent area for dining? Will more than one cook be using the cooking area at the same time? What about cleaning up? Is there room for a sink? How you use the space determines its size and layout. Likewise, placement depends not only on functionality, but on whether gas, electricity, and plumbing can be tapped into affordably.

The next decision involves the appliances. Charcoal, gas, and electric grills are all options, along with outdoor refrigerators installed underneath countertops, built-in kegs, wine coolers, and sinks with hot and cold water. Although appliances designed specifically for outdoors can withstand harsh weather conditions, adequate protection is essential, whether it's underneath a sheltered area or tucked into cabinetry.

Storage for dishes and grilling utensils simplifies outdoor cooking because everything you need is at hand. And countertop space, a given for any kitchen, will make it easier to prepare and serve food.

BELOW This deck has it all, with many of the conveniences of an indoor kitchen, including a built-in grill, sink, and refrigerator.

OPPOSITE Portable appliances and furniture designed for outdoor use can be rolled out as needed and then stored when not in use.

practical **c**onsiderations

❚ **The first rule of outdoor decorating?** Choose materials that withstand the elements. Natural materials, such as stone, wood, and stainless steel, are perennial favorites for outdoor spaces.

❚ **Attend to structural concerns** such as winterizing pipes and proper installation of appliances.

❚ **Provide ample protection** for accessories and cooking areas with a roof or an awning. Include either built-in or freestanding cabinetry to store utensils and dishes when not in use.

OPPOSITE A handsome combination of concrete, tile, stone, and stainless steel gives this patio kitchen a sleek contemporary look.

ABOVE A five-burner gas cooktop lets the homeowners cook everything from pasta to steamed vegetables outdoors.

LEFT Ice containers that are built into the concrete counter keep wine chilled.

choose a grill by price, function, and your needs

grill shopping

Bigger is not always better. Take measurements of your space before you buy to ensure the grill will fit.

Accessibility is key. Look for grills with tilt-out bins that make it easy to change the propane tank.

Electronic push-button ignitions emit a continuous spark and simplify ignition.

ABOVE This built-in grill includes side burners and storage underneath the granite counter.

OPPOSITE TOP Eliminate the need for propane tanks with a grill that is hooked into an underground gas line.

OPPOSITE BOTTOM A generous counter next to the grill is convenient for food trays and cooking utensils. This one is stone, but tile, concrete, and stainless steel are good options as well.

bright idea

accessorize

Splurge on side burners, rotisseries, and other options that make cooking outside convenient.

fireplaces and fire pits

A fireplace or fire pit may do double duty as a source for both rudimentary cooking and heat. The warm glow of an open flame is conducive to entertaining. Fireplaces are permanent structures. They anchor an outdoor space and can be a focal point for your outdoor room's design. Today's outdoor fireplaces include traditional masonry as well as prefabricated wood-burning models that can closely resemble a masonry model that has been built by hand. An outdoor gas fireplace has all of the conveniences of one that is inside your house—automatic on and off and remote control, for example.

Fire pits can be built-in or freestanding. Fire pits work well on patios, but you have to be more cautious about using one on a deck because if improperly installed it can be a fire hazard. It's important to place a fire pit on a firm, level, and noncombustible foundation. A popular option on today's market is the portable fire pit fashioned from metal or clay that rests on a metal stand.

Finally, check building regulations before installing an outdoor fireplace or fire pit, and follow the manufacturer's safety precautions.

LEFT The homeowners chose natural river rock for the face of this traditional wood-burning fireplace.

ABOVE This gas-powered unit can be operated by remote control.

OPPOSITE TOP Everyone gathers in front of this custom-built wood-burning fireplace that helps to extend the outdoor-living season through the fall.

▌

OPPOSITE BOTTOM Copper sheeting reflects the glow when this fire is lit, creating a dramatic focal point.

▌

ABOVE A clay chiminea is well suited to a small patio or terrace. Almost all chimineas burn wood.

▌

ABOVE RIGHT An outdoor heat lamp warms the air on a chilly evening.

outdoor **h**eaters

▌ **When temperatures fall**, outdoor heaters extend the season on your deck or patio. No longer for commercial use only, these heaters are generally fueled by refillable tanks but can also be tied into an existing gas line.

▌ **Place your heater** in a wind-sheltered area. You may need more than one to effectively heat a large space. Make sure a heater includes the latest safety features, such as emergency cutoff valves and flame controls.

Constructing a deck or patio often accompanies a pool or spa installation. In most cases, the pool or spa will be a focal point in the yard. Design a deck or patio to boost their functional aspects and their visual appeal. Think about how it will look as well as how it will feel underfoot.

Consider how you will use it—for sunbathing, exercising, entertaining? All three? It is also important to make accommodations for the pool's pump, filters, cleaning materials, and accessories.

pools and spas

Many spas are built-in and part of a large pool and spa design. Spa packs—the mechanical and electrical parts and the shell all within one unit—require less space and can be freestanding or set into the floor of a deck or patio. The portable units are housed in a wooden surround and require a concrete slab or a stable deck that can sustain the additional weight of the water.

OPPOSITE LEFT Nonskid tiles are a perfect material for a patio surrounding a pool.

OPPOSITE RIGHT A brick surround repeats the curvy shape of the pool here.

ABOVE A unique wooden pavilion provides partial protection from the sun.

RIGHT Decking that surrounds a pool offers an ideal place for sunbathing. A wood deck doesn't retain heat the way stone or concrete does, so you can lounge on a chaise or simply on a towel.

ABOVE A tile pool surround and patio allude to the Mediterranean inspiration for this setting.

RIGHT Rectangular pavers that have been set in a neat basket-weave pattern accent this long pool.

ABOVE Lush, dense landscaping blends this walk-in pool and patio into its surroundings.

BELOW A dramatic location, a patio, and decking provide the perfect poolside setting.

bright idea

go organic

Let the surrounding view and natural environment inspire you when you are choosing the shape of your pool.

integrate a pool with the landscape

spa maintenance and safety

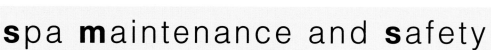

❚ **Establish a routine** to keep your spa safe and inviting. On a daily basis, make sure the spa is filled to the recommended level. Remove debris from the tub and skimmer; brush down the sides of the tub; and circulate the water.

❚ **Maintain the correct disinfectant level** of your spa and always keep the tub covered—and preferably locked—when it's not in use.

OPPOSITE This aboveground spa
has been tucked into a private corner. A few tiles next to the tub prevent grass and dirt from getting into
the water.

ABOVE A circular deck was constructed to accommodate a round
built-in spa.

LEFT The old-fashioned appeal of a
traditional hot tub adds charm to a
backyard patio.

bright idea

plant it

Some outdoor speakers look like ceramic pots or garden statuary. Search the Internet for retail sources.

While incorporating media into an exterior room is nothing new, the innovative products on today's market have elevated this aspect of outdoor living to a new level of enjoyment. For starters, these products are designed to withstand most weather conditions, which in turn enhances the functionality and flexibility of an outdoor room. Specially designed flat-screen televisions have glare shields for sunny spaces, are waterproof, and can be mounted on almost any flat surface. Some can be installed on poles and can be tilted for better viewing. When integrated with other media, they can simulate the look and feel of a home theater. CD and DVD players, radios, and tuners for outdoors are also weather resistant, as are speakers that can be installed on a wall or in the ground. And with wireless capabilities, music files can be played effortlessly whenever and wherever desired.

media

OPPOSITE TOP A TV above the fireplace lends a "lived-in" feeling to this covered patio.

OPPOSITE BOTTOM While the green ground speakers are camouflaged in the yard's bushes, their sound is clear and crisp.

ABOVE This pole-mounted TV is designed to withstand outdoor conditions, including the occasional shower from a garden hose.

Much of the fun and function of an outdoor entertaining area centers around alfresco dining. Indeed, sitting down to dinner at sunset, with a crisp breeze blowing and the air filled with the perfume of nearby flowers, creates an environment almost impossible to resist. To

dining in style

some, it is even better than dining in a five-star restaurant. To arrange such a setting in your yard, all you need is a table and comfortable seating. More elaborate decks and patios now include dedicated dining areas that are separate from other outdoor living spaces.

Whether or not your design and budget can accommodate this type of plan, make it convenient to the kitchen, unless you include an outdoor kitchen in your plans. That way, it will be so much more enjoyable if you don't have to carry heavy trays of food or drinks back and forth from indoors. Don't forget comfort: chairs or built-in benches should have cushions, and tables should be sturdy and spacious. Keep maintenance low with weather-resistant materials, such as teak or resin furniture.

TOP To keep this blonde teak ensemble handsome, use a quality wood sealer, and wash the set once a year with soap and water to remove dirt and any build up of moss.

RIGHT Lightweight aluminum and wicker chairs pair with a long table that is perfect for parties. The set is ideal for a long side yard or terrace.

OPPOSITE Here, a low table near the pool was constructed from the same wood as the deck.

ABOVE An old farm table and French café chairs re-create the look and feel of European alfresco dining.

RIGHT Durable and easy to maintain, wrought iron is a perennial favorite for outdoor dining sets. The beveled-glass top updates the look.

OPPOSITE Traditional picnic tables with a contemporary twist can be pushed together to accommodate large groups and pulled apart when a more intimate setting is desired. A retractable awning provides shade on hot, sunny afternoons.

You can enhance outdoor living on your new deck or patio with comfortable, attractive furnishings and a few special decorative accents. This chapter covers everything you need to know about pulling together a stylish outdoor design. You'll find ideas for furnishing and arranging the space, learn how to choose the right seating and dining pieces, and get tips for decorating with a particular theme in mind, including Mediterranean, English garden, modern, lake house, Zen, cabin, suburban, urban, and eclectic. Above all, you'll find the inspiration you need to create your own look.

Exterior Design

- adding flair
- seating
- dining tables
- decorating styles

The best way to make your outdoor space seem as warm and comfortable as an indoor space is to mix and match materials, textures, and colors.

One option to consider while you're planning your new deck or patio is built-in furniture, such as benches or bar tables. These items will increase the cost of your deck or patio addition, but they are space efficient—a plus when your outdoor area is limited—and permanent. Another option is free-standing outdoor furniture. Today's manufacturers provide a world of choices, including a variety of materials and styles to suit contemporary as well as traditional tastes. Some designs are in keeping with the trend toward blurring the line between exterior and interior spaces, featuring details that, until now, were found only indoors.

Durability should play a major role in your decision. Generally, outdoor furniture is made of wood, wicker, metal, plastic, or resin. Plastic or resin furniture is often lightweight and requires little care. However, metal and wood pieces that are coated with a protective finish and maintained properly will look great for years. Today's outdoor fabrics can be treated for sun, water, and mildew resistance. Rugs may be made from natural fibers, but look-alike synthetic materials hold up better. During the off-season, cover or store all of these furnishings.

adding flair

OPPOSITE A platform bed is a natural fit in this Zen-inspired garden. The fabrics and cushions are manufactured for outdoor use, but you may want to protect them from rain.

ABOVE An ultramodern outdoor "office" features an industrial-inspired stainless-steel desk and chair.

bright idea

cushions

You can re-cover most cushions, but use fabric that is coated for outdoor use. Even if you just spot-treat old cushions, spray them with fabric protector.

furnish your outdoor room with style ||||||||||||||||||||||||||||

OPPOSITE TOP   Elegant chaise longues add style to a poolside patio.

OPPOSITE BOTTOM   Improved finishes keep outdoor furniture looking good all season.

ABOVE   With comfortable furnishings, this covered deck becomes an open-air living room.

judging quality

Just as you would examine a piece of furniture for inside your home, carefully look over any pieces you are considering for the deck or patio. Shake the furniture to check for sturdiness, inspect the joints, and make sure that there are no protruding fasteners or jagged edges. Evaluate finishes by their ability to repel water and resist scratching. For fabrics, look for heavyweight materials and special coatings designed to deflect and deter ultraviolet rays, moisture, mildew, and fading.

OPPOSITE Outdoor furniture can be as comfortable as anything you have inside your home. Quality pieces can hold up almost year-round in most climates, too.

ABOVE This multipurpose console houses a fire pit, has a stone surface for resting a drink, and offers storage behind the cabinet doors.

BELOW Sleek lines and natural wood define this chair. In a garden setting, it looks like a piece of art.

Small pleasures, such as reading a book on your deck or having drinks with friends on the patio, are made all the more enjoyable when you have comfortable, ample seating. Arrange sofas and chairs in a layout conducive to conversation.

seating

Transform a cozy corner into an impromptu dining area. Add a chaise longue or even a daybed for an afternoon siesta.

Decks often feature built-in seating. If you choose to include it in your design, ask the builder to increase the comfort of these pieces by slanting the backs of built-in benches and making the seats at least 15 inches deep for good lumbar support.

Even if you opt for built-in seating, you'll want stylish portable pieces that you can arrange or move as needed. Your choices will include chairs, gliders, rockers, sofas, chaise longues, club chairs, and stools. Try them out in the showroom, evaluating them for comfort and sturdiness. Unless protected, furniture with intricate parts and ornate woodwork are not suitable for outdoor use because mold, mildew, and outdoor elements can easily work their way into crevices and mechanical parts. Seat cushions will last longer when they are made from acrylic filling and weather- and ultraviolet-resistant fabric.

BELOW A table and chairs dressed in pretty linens and cushions make this patio comfortable and inviting.

OPPOSITE A rustic twig chair is the perfect piece for a casual deck. Applying a weatherproof sealant every other year will keep it in top shape.

built-in seating can be sophisticated

ABOVE Striped bolsters and flat seat cushions dress up these built-in banquettes.

OPPOSITE An aluminum bistro table and chairs can be drawn up to the banquette for dining.

LEFT Colorful throw pillows soften the angular lines and the hard landing of concrete seating.

ABOVE Natural twig and reed chairs are charming but delicate. Protect them from the weather or use them only in covered areas.

RIGHT Easy to store, lightweight, and washable butterfly chairs with removable canvas covers are practical and stylish on the patio.

seating styles

There are several types of seating that are suitable for outdoor use:

▍**Cushion seating** has a cushion that fits on top of a frame. The cushions can be removed for cleaning.

▍**Sling seating** has one piece of fabric secured to a frame to form a seat. It dries quickly and holds its shape.

▍**Strap seating** features woven strips of plastic or canvas secured to the chair frame.

▍**Vinyl-mesh seating** is woven plastic used for portable beach chairs.

BELOW A modular ensemble with a cypress frame is naturally resistant to water and insects.

OPPOSITE TOP Teak chaise longues with removable cushions can be folded easily and stored over the winter.

OPPOSITE BOTTOM This hammock in an unusual teak frame is a focal point of this deck.

bright idea

wood

Cypress and teak are harder and more weather-resistant than other types of wood, and can be left untreated to weather naturally.

wood blends naturally into outdoor spaces |||||||||||||||||||

dining tables

A dining table for your deck or patio should meet the same criteria as one you would choose to use indoors—it has to be the right size for both your family and your new outdoor space. If you entertain often, look for a table that is expandable. Otherwise, think about using two or more small tables that you can group together for intimate gatherings or place around the patio or deck when you're having large parties.

Standard dining tables are 32 inches high, but countertop-height (36 inches) and bar-table-height models (40 inches) are options.

Any dining table should be sturdy—if it wobbles in the showroom, don't buy it. Wiggle the table's legs to check for looseness at the joints, and examine the finish for scratches or imperfections.

The most durable outdoor tables are made from the right wood—teak and cypress weather well—and given a protective finish. Others, such as wrought iron, glass, aluminum, plastic, or resin, are popular, too. Whatever, you chose, proper cleaning and storage over the winter will keep your furniture in good shape. Besides a dining table, buffets, portable bars, and food prep stations simplify entertaining.

OPPOSITE A long table that seats eight will be adequate for most families. A teak table, such as this one, should be oiled to preserve its color. Left to weather naturally, it will turn a silvery gray.

BELOW An oval table will seat more people comfortably. This one has a plastic surface and matching chairs. To clean the set, use a damp cloth and a mild detergent.

LEFT This painted wrought-iron set is pretty, but it may get hot or be uncomfortable when sitting for long periods of time, so add cushions to the chairs.

OPPOSITE Black wrought iron and glass are a classic combination. Striped cushions in green and white make this spot inviting.

room for **c**omfort

Less is more, especially if your patio or deck is compact. For limited spaces, choose furniture with a dual purpose, such as a daybed that also works as a settee or sofa. Provide ample room for sliding chairs in and out from a table. Keep high-traffic areas open and unimpeded by furniture. And consider issues like good lighting, floor surfaces, and accessories to make your outdoor space comfortable, safe, and welcoming.

Outdoor living has always been fun, but never so much as it is now. Because it's more popular than ever, designers and manufacturers are providing ideas and furnishings that let you create indoor sophistication outdoors. Have a favorite decorating style for

decorating styles

your home's interior spaces? Carry it outdoors—or go for a look that's entirely different. There are no rules to follow, but you could take cues from the size and shape of the deck or patio to help you make the most of the space when you're choosing furniture. You might also consider what you can see of the space from inside your home, especially if you have large windows or glass doors that offer a view. Indoor and outdoor decor doesn't have to match, but colors and styles that coordinate will make the overall look cohesive.

With all of this in mind, you can choose your colors, furniture, and decorating style with confidence. Turn to sources such as magazines and showhouses for ideas, pulling together images of those you particularly like. When you have a representative sample, begin picking and choosing from each to create your own look. It is also helpful to look at rug, paint, and fabric swatches outdoors, checking the palette in natural light.

OPPOSITE Natural wicker furniture, toss pillows, and a jute rug make this country patio comfortable.

LEFT A small table and chairs add a cozy French-bistro look to this corner.

BELOW Vibrant printed fabrics from Mexico dress up this outdoor dining area.

bright idea

Mediterranean

A stucco
fireplace or pizza
oven adds a taste of
Italy to the outdoors.
Some are available
as kits with a
choice of
finishes.

sun-washed colors have old-world appeal

OPPOSITE Columns, ironwork, and natural stone add instant "age" to this new outdoor space.

ABOVE Natural, earthy materials are the signature of Mediterranean style.

RIGHT Lush plantings around the patio are reminiscient of places near the sea. The hand-painted ceramic dishes are imported from Italy.

BELOW Lots of container plants and garden furniture set the style here. Clay tiles are practical for places where you will be repotting and watering plants.

OPPOSITE It's tea time on the patio. Surrounded by a garden, this outdoor spot has all the charm of the English countryside. A few vintage serving pieces enhance the effect.

bright idea

English garden

The charm of a traditional English garden can be emulated by adding a cozy dining set and surrounding it with flowers and foliage.

flowers and fragrance define English garden style

well-edited rooms characterize a modern aesthetic

LEFT An unpretentious flower border on two sides of this limestone-tile patio contrasts with the ultra-modern and starkly white plastic chairs and table, softening their look. A plastic carafe and glasses in lime green add punch.

BELOW This low resin table and benches have all the right lines and angles for a modern design. Tall blue flowers in the adjacent planting bed pick up the cobalt color of the furniture.

bright idea
modern times
Organic and linear structures play an limportant role in modern design. Balance them by choosing complemen-tary materials and keeping details to a minimum.

ABOVE A simple pine bed surrounded by trees turns this covered deck into the perfect summer sleeping loft.

OPPOSITE TOP A cozy chaise is the perfect perch for watching boats sail by on the lake.

OPPOSITE BOTTOM Handsome high-back chairs have been stained to match the color of the deck and natural siding.

▍ informality and woodsy hues enhance this look ▍▐▍▐▍▐▍▐▍▐▍

bright idea

lake house

Keep it simple and unpretentious. Let the trees and shoreline views inspire your lake-house decorating style.

bright idea

zen

Order and simplicity connote Zen style. Because the look is minimalist, it goes well with modern architecture and furniture. This combination is sometimes called "fushion design."

create a calm, uncluttered style

TOP A proper altar in a Zen garden includes a representation of the Buddha.

ABOVE Minimal design, typified by these chairs, fuses well with the Zen look.

OPPOSITE Order is a key element in achieving "enlightened" design.

bright idea

cabin

Indigenous materials, rough finishes, and comfortable touches are typical of cabin style. Avoid overdecorating and use colors from nature.

⫿⫿ relaxed, rustic, and warm—that's cabin style ⫿⫿⫿⫿⫿⫿⫿⫿⫿⫿⫿⫿⫿⫿

OPPOSITE TOP A bentwood chair, often made out of hickory, has a one-of-a-kind look.

OPPOSITE BOTTOM A simple, earthy palette brings out the best here.

ABOVE Log furniture is the perfect choice for cabin style. These pieces have been crafted from cedar.

bright idea

suburban

Comfortable, durable designs that cater to family and friends could include furniture crafted of man-made "wicker." This product looks great and stands up to the weather.

ABOVE Group seating pieces to give a large patio an intimate "family room" feeling.

OPPOSITE TOP LEFT Separate the dining area from the rest of the space with a covering or partition.

OPPOSITE TOP RIGHT Create a container garden on your deck. Mix flowers with vegetables and herbs.

OPPOSITE BOTTOM Paint patio furniture to match the house for a seamless indoor-outdoor transition.

create family-friendly, yet chic design

OPPOSITE One designer created a backyard urban oasis with decking, container plants, and unique fountains.

BELOW An Adirondack chair looks comfortably at home on this city terrace. The natural wood of the furniture and the decking is a warm contrast to the concrete wall.

city retreats can be urbane or plain |||||||||||||||||||||||||

bright idea

Urban

Form follows function, and in urban environments, outdoor rooms must be multifunctional because they are usually limited in size.

LEFT Use multiple fabric prints, but choose one unifying element, such as pattern, color, or motif.

BELOW Vintage wrought-iron doors are hinged to create a New Orleans-style backdrop or screen for this corner room. Handmade quilts add color.

OPPOSITE This patio incorporates elements of several styles, including touches of French bistro, cottage, and modern.

anything goes with the spontaneous look of eclectic

bright idea

eclectic

The main principle for eclectic style is to combine the colors, styles, furniture, and fabrics you like. There's no right or wrong way—let your intuition guide your choices.

8

The effects of outdoor lighting are obvious. It transforms your deck or patio into a place for dining, relaxing, or entertaining long after the sun has set. Just as important, it can evoke a mood. Few settings are as magical as a garden at night, and when careful thought is put into the placement and the type of light, that magic is enhanced. This chapter will explore various kinds of outdoor lighting options and fixtures, including tips for installation and placement that will maximize the function and decor of your new outdoor room and yard.

Outdoor Lighting

- planning
- the right fixture

Lighting is practical, but it can be decorative, too. In this case, a large pendant provides good overall light while helping to coordinate all of the modern furnishings.

P atios and decks are places to relax and catch up with family and friends after a busy day. Especially during the summer, people often prefer to spend evenings at home outdoors. To maximize use, your deck or patio should have lighting that takes into consideration your activities.

General, task, and accent lighting—the same types that are necessary for optimizing

planning

your interior spaces—can enhance your outdoor-living experience. Begin by deciding where you need light, keeping in mind that too much direct light can be harsh and unattractive. Walkways and stairs should be well lit; brick lights inserted into walls near the stairs, fixtures that can be tucked under deck railings, sconces, and post lamps all provide general illumination for high-traffic areas. Look for fixtures that coordinate with your house style.

Position task lights near activity zones: the food preparation and cooking area, wet bar, or wherever you plan to set up drinks and snacks while entertaining.

A dining table and conversation benefit from soft light, and candles can be ideal for setting just the right glow.

Accent lighting can create a mood or call attention to handsome architecture or landscaping features. Add drama by uplighting or backlighting shrubbery, or by moonlighting a tree—casting light down from several points. Position a spotlight to focus on a garden ornament or a fountain. These are just a few examples. Finally, vary your lighting techniques for maximum impact.

OPPOSITE Strategically placed spotlights cast a directed glow at various points on this deck.

LEFT Candles and oil lamps create their own special mood. However, use them with caution.

BELOW Dramatic lighting design plays up both light and shadows.

bright idea
light the grill

Many of today's outdoor living areas are designed around grills or entire kitchens. For convenience and safety, make sure to include general and task lighting in your plans for this space.

ABOVE LEFT Recessed compact halogen fixtures provide suitable general illumination for this outdoor kitchen and patio.

LEFT Small spotlights hidden in the plant bed illuminate plantings and artwork in this modern outdoor space.

OPPOSITE At night, this design relies on multiple light sources, such as the Noguchi-style pendant and numerous spotlights, as well as several lighting techniques—uplighting and wall washing—for its sophisticated look.

accent lighting

The beauty of accent lighting is that it can be directed specifically to highlight certain elements or features. Although it does not provide overall illumination, it can help to brighten a path or stairs at night.

Spotlights can be broad in their reach (think floodlights) or tightly focused on a particular feature for emphasis. Wall washing casts a warm glow over a wall, floor, or outdoor feature, such as a fountain or trellis.

OPPOSITE TOP Carefully placed lighting enhances the texture on these panels.

OPPOSITE BOTTOM With evenly spaced uplights, this wall becomes a backdrop for the silhouetted form of the grasses and other plantings.

ABOVE Hang lanterns in a tree or scatter them around the garden for a pretty effect at night.

LEFT Light changes the intensity and depth of the color here.

BELOW LEFT If you expect to use your patio or deck at night, consider the evening view. Place a spotlight underneath a tree to create a focal point in the yard.

BELOW RIGHT Lighting that simulates moon glow adds mystery and romance to a garden. Use light creatively outdoors for a unique decorative effect.

OPPOSITE The juxtaposition of water and light can evoke a magical feeling. Including a water feature on or near your patio or deck will increase your enjoyment of the space.

bright idea

you can do it

Low-voltage lighting fixtures that are designed especially for decks are easy to install.

LEFT A corrugated metal wall reflects light from the small fixtures beautifully.

ABOVE Recessed in the brick wall, compact lights brighten the stairs unobtrusively.

OPPOSITE In addition to its practical purpose, the lighting built under these stair treads is decorative.

responsible **l**ighting

Low-voltage lighting is eco-friendly. First, it conserves energy (and is less costly to operate). In addition, many manufacturers have introduced "dark sky" shield accessories that avoid night-sky pollution, complying with related ordinances that are being enacted across the country.

| | | | | | | | | | artful lighting draws attention to details | | | | | | | | | |

ABOVE Highlighted by tiny spotlights installed in the deck floor, the texture and patina of old brick lends character to an otherwise ordinary space.

|

RIGHT Pin lights that have been installed within the boards are barely visible but they are a necessary safety feature.

|

OPPOSITE Simple canisters provide housing for lights that dramatize the organic forms and textures in this Zen garden.

the right fixture

Y ou can find the perfect fixture to suit your deck or patio lighting needs. Take style cues from your home's architecture and existing fixtures. Generally speaking, brass, bronze, copper, and wrought iron tend to be more traditional than stainless steel, nickel, or chrome, but none of these are exclusive to any one look today. You can find renderings of fixtures in all of these materials that will coordinate with almost any style.

Although satin or antique finishes are most popular, polished versions are readily available for those who prefer a glossy look.

Landscape lighting is often utilitarian, blending unobtrusively into the landscape so that the light—not the fixture—is noticed. However, some fixtures, such as sconces and pendants, are decorative and meant to be seen.

When purchasing outdoor lighting, check to be sure the fixtures are UL listed for use in wet or damp locations. Cast-aluminum fixtures suffice for most applications, but those made of marine-grade alloy aluminum, die-cast brass, solid copper, and rugged composites are the most durable. Look for porcelain bulb bases and designs that make it easy to replace bulbs. When possible, use energy-saving low-voltage or fluorescent lamps.

OPPOSITE Anodized aluminum and contemporary styling distinguish this outdoor fixture.

ABOVE Custom-designed rectangular metal columns serve as planters while housing low-voltage landscape lights.

RIGHT It's safe to walk on these lights, which are designed to be mounted flush with the deck floor. You can install them on stair treads, too.

ABOVE Small tea lights illuminate these patio lanterns and set the mood for an early evening dinner party outdoors.

ABOVE RIGHT A handsome fixture can be an attractive accent in a flower bed.

RIGHT Flexible LED strip lights can be cut to any length, stay cool, and are long lasting. They're an interesting accent on this deck floor.

OPPOSITE Industrial-inspired fixtures line this pathway with sleek, modern styling.

energy **s**mart

▌**Energy-efficient, compact-fluorescent lights (CFLs)** last longer than standard incandescent ones, so it makes sense to use them outdoors. But make sure it has a cold-weather ballast if you live in an area that doesn't stay warm year-round.

▌**Lamps powered by small photovoltaic (PV) modules** are another energy-efficient option. This type of device converts sunlight into electricity. If your deck or patio is located too far from your power source, you might consider this alternative.

bright idea

keep it simple

Waterfalls or fountains will sparkle when you direct lights toward them from the pond edges. Also, some fountain systems include underwater lights.

LEFT Light coming from a source on the wall above the fountain highlights both the brick and the water.

ABOVE Artful lighting draws attention to the statuary and the pavilion beyond it.

OPPOSITE TOP The pond's underwater lights illuminate the fountains, while uplights dramatize the craggy rocks that surround it.

RIGHT At night, underwater lighting transforms this backyard waterfall into a shimmering wall.

enhance a water feature with light

9

A water feature can be a dynamic element in your design. The sights and sounds of a fountain, waterfall, or a pond can increase the pleasure of being outdoors, adding beauty to your at-home escape both day and night. For some projects, you may need to call a plumber or an electrician, but not every installation is complex. Some fountains—both tabletop and full-size versons—simply plug into an outdoor electrical outlet. Before you get too far along with your deck or patio plans, consider a water feature. But don't forget to think carefully about its placement, safety, support, and style.

Water Features

▌ fountains and waterfalls

The soothing sound of cascading water boosts this deck's relaxation quotient.

fountains and waterfalls

A fountain or waterfall near, if not on, your new deck or patio can add the calming sound of moving water to your outdoor experience while buffering unwanted street noises. It can be an attractive focal point, too, tying together various exterior design elements, or it can reinforce a particular theme or architectural style.

A fountain can be either freestanding or wall mounted. Either way, it will require a power source to run the pump's motor. Fountains of all styles come in two basic types: spray fountains (water nozzles or jets that spray water in different patterns) and statuary fountains.

Waterfalls usually consist of a series of small pools or catch basins linked by low cascades. Constructing one is more complex than adding a fountain. It involves both art and engineering. If your space is limited, a single raised basin that empties into a pond, or a springlike gush from a fissure in a rock wall or ledge above a small pond may still produce the effect you desire.

OPPOSITE Adding a narrow nozzle to the pipe will give your fountain a tall "geyser" spray.

LEFT Most spray fountains come as complete kits. This fountain's spray pattern is called an "inverted cone."

MIDDLE Here's a sleek, modern design for a patio: a single, wide sheet of water cascades from the wall into a raised pond.

BOTTOM This illustrates how some of the best designs are the simplest. A small hole empties water from a raised waterway into a low basin.

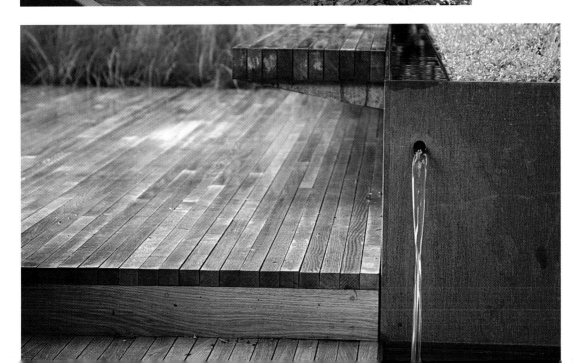

plug in the pump and just add water

OPPOSITE TOP Size is key to selecting the right fountain for your deck or patio. This stone fountain is big on impact but takes up little space.

OPPOSITE BOTTOM Hand-crafted from metal and installed on a tile patio, this fountain provides contemporary contrast to the more traditional look of the country garden.

ABOVE A compact, low fountain with a bell-shaped spray fits snugly into a flower bed, but you could tuck a similar one into a border surrounding a patio.

ABOVE A do-it-yourself kit transformed an oversize clay teapot, cup, and saucer into a whimsical water feature.

RIGHT Careful planning is required for this formal design.

OPPOSITE This sphere-shaped design was formed in concrete.

most spray fountains come as kits

||||||statuary fountains are often made of precast concrete ||

ABOVE Animal heads and feet are common themes in garden statuary. The wall fountain is based on a classic design.

RIGHT This whimsical idea is part of a miniature container pond created in a barrel. Its size makes it perfect for even a small deck or patio.

OPPOSITE TOP A gargoyle is a Gothic figure that is often used as a waterspout.

OPPOSITE BOTTOM An architecturally classic design features a carved-mask variation on the Medieval "Green Man."

Resource Guide

Alcoa Home Exteriors

201 Isabella St.

Pittsburgh, PA 15212-5858

800-962-6973

www.alcoa.com/alcoahomes

Manufactures aluminum and synthetic building materials, including deck products under the Oasis brand.

Alumatec Industries Inc.

529 Orange Ave.

Daytona, FL 32114

800-989-7245

www.alumatecindustries.com

Manufactures and installs a complete line of aluminum, stainless-steel, and brass railings.

Andersen Corp.

100 Fourth Ave. N.

Bayport, MN 55003-1096

800-426-4261

www.andersenwindows.com

Offers a full line of patio doors and windows.

APA – The Engineered Wood Association

7011 S. Nineteenth St.

Tacoma, WA 98466

253-565-6600

www.apawood.org

A nonprofit trade association that produces a variety of engineered wood products.

AridDek

1604 Athens Hwy.

Gainesville, GA 30507

877-270-9387

www.ariddek.com

Manufactures aluminum decking and railings.

AZEK Trimboards

801 Corey St.

Moosic, PA 18507

877-275-2935

www.azek.com

Offers synthetic trim products, including balustrades, moldings, and lattice skirting.

Beuchel Stone Corp.

W3639 Hwy. H

Chilton, WI 53014

800-236-4473

www.buechelstone.com

Provides natural, quarried stone from select cities. Its product line includes patio stone, accent boulders, and custom-cut stones for stairs.

Blue Rhino Corp.

104 Cambridge Plaza Dr.

Winston-Salem, NC 27104

800-762-1142

www.uniflame.com

Offers a full line of grills, heaters, and other outdoor appliances, and a propane tank exchange program.

CableRail/Feeney Architectural Products

2603 Union St.

Oakland, CA 94607

800-888-2418

www.cablerail.com

Manufactures a line of standard and custom stainless-steel cable assemblies.

The following list of manufacturers and associations is meant to be a general guide to additional industry and product-related sources. It is not intended as a listing of products and manufacturers represented by the photographs in this book.

California Redwood Association

405 Enfrente Dr., Ste. 200

Novato, CA 94949-7206

888-225-7339

www.calredwood.org

Offers technical information about the use of redwood for decks and other structures.

Cascades

404 Marie-Victorin Blvd.

Kingsey Falls, QC, Canada J0A 1B0

819-363-5100

www.cascades.com

A packaging product firm that also makes decking from recycled plastic under the Perma-deck brand.

Cecco Trading, Inc.

600 E. Vienna Ave.

Milwaukee, WI 53212

414-445-8989

www.ironwoods.com

Supplies the Iron Wood brand of Ipe hardwood lumber.

The Colonial Stoneyard

66 North St.

Groton, MA 01450

978-448-3329

www.colonialstoneyard.com

Specializes in natural stone and stone products for landscaping projects.

Concrete Foundations Association

107 First St. W.

P.O. Box 204

Mount Vernon, IA 52314

319-895-6940

www.cfawalls.org

Provides educational materials to contractors in 26 states and Canada.

Correct Building Products

8 Morin St.

Biddeford, ME 04005

877-332-5877

www.correctdeck.com

Maker of CorrectDeck, a composite decking material.

Deck Images

12590 127th St. S.

Hastings, MN 55033

877-446-7397

www.deckimages.com

Manufactures powder-coated aluminum and glass railing systems for residential and commercial markets.

Deckmaster

205 Mason Cir.

Concord, CA 94520

800-869-1375

www.deckmaster.com

Makes bracket-style hidden deck fasteners.

Resource Guide

Deckorators
50 Crestwood Executive Center, Ste. 308
Crestwood, MO 63126
800-332-5724
www.deckorators.com
Manufactures a wide range of aluminum balustrades and glass railings in many colors and designs.

DekBrands
P.O. Box 14804
Minneapolis, MN 55414
800-664-2705
www.deckplans.com
Manufacturers deck systems.

DESA
2701 Industrial Dr.
Bowling Green, KY 42101
866-672-6040
www.desatech.com
Manufactures security lights and deck heaters.

Dry-B-Lo
475 Tribble Gap Rd., Ste. 305
Cumming, GA 30040
800-437-9256
www.dry-b-lo.com
Manufactures aluminum deck drainage systems.

EB-TY Hidden Deck-Fastening Systems
Blue Heron Enterprises, LLC
P.O. Box 5389
North Branch, NJ 08876
800-438-3289
www.ebty.com
Makes biscuit-style hidden deck fasteners.

EverGrain Composite Decking, a div. of TAMKO Building Products, Inc.
P.O. Box 1404
Joplin, MO 64802
800-253-1401
www.evergrain.com
Manufactures composite decking products with realistic, compression-molded graining patterns.

Forest Stewardship Council-U.S.
1155 30th St. NW, Ste. 300
Washington, D.C. 20007
202-342-0413
www.fscus.org
A nonprofit organization devoted to encouraging the responsible management of the world's forests.

Gaco Western

P.O. Box 88698

Seattle, WA 98138

866-422-6489

www.gaco.com

Manufactures a high-quality acrylic polymer waterproof surface protection for plywood or plank decks.

Gale Pacific

P.O. Box 951509

Lake Mary, FL 32795-1509

800-560-4667

www.coolaroo.com

Manufactures a wide range of outdoor fabrics with various degrees of UV protection.

Grace Construction Products

62 Whittemore Ave.

Cambridge, MA 02140

800-354-5414

www.graceconstruction.com

www.graceathome.com

Offers self-adhering flashing for decks.

Hadco Lighting, a div. of Genlyte Group Inc.

100 Craftway

Littlestown, PA 17340

800-331-4185

www.hadcolighting.com

Offers a large variety of outdoor lighting designed for decks, including post, step, path, and area lights.

Hearth & Home Technologies

20802 Kensington Blvd.

Lakeville, MN 55044

888-669-4328

www.hearthnhome.com

Offers a complete line of gas, electric, and wood-burning heating products.

Hearth, Patio, and Barbecue Association (HPBA)

1601 N. Kent St., Ste. 1001

Arlington, VA 22209

703-522-0086

www.hpba.org

Promotes the hearth-products industry.

Highpoint Deck Lighting

P.O. Box 428

Black Hawk, CO 80422

888-582-5850

www.hpdlighting.com

Produces a full line of outdoor lighting, including railing lights, recessed stair lights, hanging lanterns, wall sconces, and barbecue cook lights.

Hooks and Lattice

5671 Palmer Way, Ste. K

Carlsbad, CA 92010

800-896-0978

www.hooksandlattice.com

Web site features all styles of window boxes designed for every application, including deck railings.

International Masonry Institute

The James Brice House

42 East St.

Annapolis, MD 21401

410-280-1305

www.imiweb.org

Provides marketing materials for the masonry industry.

Resource Guide

Jacuzzi
14525 Monte Vista Ave.
Chino, CA 91710
866-234-7727
www.jacuzzi.com
Manufactures a full line of hot tubs and deck spas.

Learning Stone
www.learningstone.net
Offers a number of links to various stone resources.

LockDry
FSI Home Products Division
2700 Alabama Hwy. 69 S.
Cullman, AL 35057
800-711-1785
www.lockdry.com
Manufactures patented aluminum deck and railing systems with built-in continuous gutters.

Marvin Windows and Doors
P.O. Box 100
Warroad, MN 56763
888-537-7828
www.marvin.com
Makers of a full line of windows and doors, including sliders and French doors.

Masonry Advisory Council
1480 Renaissance Dr., Ste. 302
Park Ridge, IL 60068
847-297-6704
www.maconline.org
Provides the public with general and technical information about masonry design and detail.

NanaWall Systems, Inc.
707 Redwood Hwy.
Mill Valley, CA 94941
800-873-5673
www.nanawall.com
Manufactures folding wall systems of easy-to-open glass panels.

National Fenestration Rating Council (NFRC)
8484 Georgia Ave., Ste. 320
Silver Spring, MD 20910
301-589-1776
www.nfrc.org
A nonprofit organization that administers the only uniform, independent rating and labeling system for the energy performance of patio doors and other products.

Pella Corporation
102 Main St.
Pella, IA 50219
800-374-4758
www.pella.com
Manufactures energy-efficient patio doors and windows.

Procell Decking Systems
11746 Foley Beach Express
Foley, AL 36535
251-943-2916
www.procelldeck.com
Manufactures synthetic stain- and scratch-resistant decking from PVC.

Progress Lighting
P.O. Box 5704
Spartanburg, SC 29304-5704
864-599-6000

www.progresslighting.com

Makes wall lanterns that have motion detectors built into the mounting plate or the lantern itself, as well as deck and landscape lights.

Punch! Software, LLC

7900 NW 100th St., Ste. LL6

Kansas City, MO 64153

800-365-4832

www.punchsoftware.com

Software company specializing in home and landscaping design programs.

Royal Crown Limited

P.O. Box 360

Milford, IN 46542-0360

800-488-5245

www.royalcrownltd.com

Produces vinyl deck planks and railing products under the Triple Crown Fence, Brock Deck Systems, Brock Deck, and Deck Lok Systems brands.

Select Stone, Inc.

P.O. Box 6403

Bozeman, MT 59771

888-237-1000

www.selectstone.com

Source for natural stone from the United States, as well as Europe and Asia. The company provides stone to residential and commercial construction projects throughout the United States.

Shade Sails LLC

7028 Greenleaf Ave., Ste. K

Whittier, CA 90602

562-945-9952

www.shadesails.com

Imports tensioned, UV-treated fabric canopies.

ShadeScapes USA

39300 Back River Rd.

Paonia, CO 81428

866-997-4233

www.shadescapesusa.com

Manufactures side- and center-post shade umbrellas.

Southern Pine Council

2900 Indiana Ave.

Kenner, LA 70065-4605

504-443-4464

www.southernpine.com

A trade association that offers information on building decks with treated lumber.

Starborn Industries, Inc.

27 Engelhard Ave.

Avenel, NJ 07001

800-596-7747

www.starbornindustries.com

Manufactures stainless-steel deck-fastening systems, including Headcote- and DeckFast-brand screws.

Summer Classics

P.O. Box 390

7000 Hwy. 25

Montevallo, AL 35115

205-987-3100

www.summerclassics.com

Manufactures deck and garden furnishings in wrought aluminum, wrought iron, and woven resin.

Resource Guide

Summerwood Products

735 Progress Ave.

Toronto, ON, Canada M1H 2W7

866-519-4634

www.summerwood.com

Offers prefab customized kits for outdoor structures, such as gazebos, pool cabanas, and spa enclosures.

Sundance Spas

14525 Monte Vista Ave.

Chino, CA 91710

800-883-7727

www.sundancespas.com

The largest manufacturer of acrylic spas.

Sustainable Forestry Initiative

American Forest & Paper Association

1111 Nineteenth St. NW, Ste. 800

Washington, D.C. 20036

www.aboutsfi.org

A comprehensive forestry management program developed by the American Forest & Paper Association.

TAMKO Building Products, Inc.

EverGrain Composite Decking

Elements Decking

220 W. Fourth St.

Joplin, MO 64801

800-641-4691

www.tamko.com

www.evergrain.com

www.elementsdecking.com

Manufactures composite decking products using compression molding for a real-wood look.

Tiger Claw Inc.

400 Middle St., Ste. J

Bristol, CT 06010-8405

800-928-4437

www.deckfastener.com

Manufactures products for the construction industry, including hidden deck fasteners.

TimberTech

894 Prairie Ave.

Wilmington, OH 45177

800-307-7780

www.timbertech.com

Manufacturers composite decking and railing systems, fascia boards, and specialty trim.

Timber Treatment Technologies

8700 Trail Lake Dr., Ste. 101

Germantown, TN 38125

866-318-9432

www.timbersil.com

Developer of a new process for preserving wood. The nontoxic and noncorrosive formula is designed for both aboveground and in-ground applications.

Trex Company, Inc.

160 Exeter Dr.

Winchester, VA 22603

800-289-8739

www.trex.com

Manufatures composite decking materials.

Universal Forest Products, Inc.

2801 E. Beltline Ave. NE

Grand Rapids, MI 49525

616-364-6161

www.ufpi.com

Manufactures and distributes wood and wood-alternative products for decking and railing systems.

Western Red Cedar Lumber Association (WRCLA)

1501-700 W. Pender St.

Pender Place 1, Business Building

Vancouver, BC, Canada V6C 1G8

866-778-9096

www.realcedar.org

www.wrcla.org

www.cedar-deck.org

A nonprofit trade association representing quality producers of western red cedar in the United States and Canada.

Weyerhaeuser Co.

P.O. Box 1237

Springdale, AR 72765

800-951-5117

www.choicedek.com

Manufactures ChoiceDek-brand decking from a blend of low- and high-density polyethylene plastic and wood fibers. Also distributes CedarOne cedar decking.

Wolman Wood Care Products, a div. of Zinsser Co., Inc.

173 Belmont Dr.

Somerset, NJ 08875

800-556-7737

www.wolman.com

Makes products used to restore, beautify, and protect decks and other exterior wood structures.

Glossary

Accent lighting: Lighting that highlights a surface or object to emphasize its character.

Aggregate: Crushed stone, gravel, or other material added to cement to make concrete or mortar. Gravel and crushed stone are considered coarse aggregate.

Arbor: A freestanding wooden structure upon which vines are grown to create a shady retreat.

Ashlar: Any stone cut to a square or rectangular shape in either random or uniform sizes. Also, a pattern for laying courses of rectangular blocks of stone.

Awning: A roof-like structure, often made of weather-resistant canvas or plastic, that's attached to an exterior wall to provide shelter.

Backfill: Sand, gravel, pea stone, or crushed stone used to refill excavated areas with a stable, porous material.

Balusters: The vertical pieces, generally made of 2x2s, that fill the spaces between rails and posts to create a guardrail.

Balustrade: A guardrail, often used around the perimeter of a deck, consisting of balusters, posts, and top and bottom rails.

Beam: The term for any large horizontal framing member.

Bed: Horizontal masonry joint, sometimes called bed joint. Also, any prepared surface (stone, gravel, sand, or mortar) for placing stone.

Belgian blocks: Stone cut in square or rectangular shapes, usually about the size of a large brick, and used for paving.

Blind fasteners: Clips, brackets, or biscuits used to fasten decking to joists in such a way as to be hidden from view. An alternative to top-driven nails and screws.

Building codes: Municipal rules regulating safe building practices and procedures. Generally, the codes encompass structural, electrical, plumbing, and mechanical remodeling and new construction.

Building permit: An authorization to build or renovate according to plans approved by the local building department. Generally, any job that includes a footing or foundation or that involves any structural work requires a permit.

Built-in: Any element, such as a bench or planter, that is attached permanently to the deck.

Cantilever: Construction that extends horizontally beyond its support.

Clearance: The amount of recommended space between two fixtures,

such as between a grill and railing. Some clearances may be mandated by building codes.

Cobblestone: Any small-dimension milled stone that is used for paving.

Column: A supporting pillar consisting of a base, a cylindrical shaft, and a capital.

Composite: Building materials, including deck planking and railings, that are made by combining wood waste or fiber with plastics.

Concrete: A mixture of portland cement, sand, gravel or crushed rock, and water that forms a solid material when cured.

Cornice: A horizontal molding that projects from the top of a wall to create a finished or decorative appearance.

Crazy paving: Irregularly shaped pieces of stone used to make a walk or patio.

Crushed rock: Small-dimension material available in a range of colors and sizes with rough, angular surfaces.

Curing: The process by which concrete becomes solid and develops strength.

Cut stone: Any stone that has been milled or worked by hand to a specific shape or dimensions.

Decay-resistant woods: Woods, such as redwood and cedar, that are naturally resistant to rot.

Decking: Boards fastened to joists to form the deck surface.

Dressed stone: Usually quarried stone that has been squared-off on all sides and has a smooth face.

Eave: The lower edge of a roof that overhangs a wall.

Excavation: To remove earth or soil so that the construction will be supported by a subgrade that is hard, uniformly graded, and well drained.

Exposure: Contact with the sun's rays, wind, and inclement weather.

Fascia: Horizontal boards that cover the joint between the top of an exterior wall and its eaves.

Fieldstone: Stone as it is found in the natural environment.

Fire pit: A built-in masonry well, typically built into the center of the deck, used to contain a fire. Some portable metal hearths are also called fire pits.

Flagging: Paving for walks or patios made from flagstone.

Flagstone: Any stone milled to a uniform thickness of 1 to 2 inches to use for walk and patio surfaces. Flagstone is available in uniform rectangular shapes or in random-shaped pieces sometimes called crazy paving.

Floodlights: Outdoor lights with strong, bright beams used for security or to highlight a large object, such as an arbor or tree.

Fluting: A decorative motif consisting of a series of parallel, uniform grooves.

Focal point: A design term for the dominant visual element in a space.

Footing: A concrete pad, usually at the frost line, that supports posts, piers, or stairs.

Frost line: The maximum depth at which soil freezes in a given locale. Footings generally must sit below the frost line in colder climates or else heaving, due to water in soil freezing, can cause structural instability.

Gazebo: A framed structure with a peaked roof that is usually octagonal. Gazebos offer protection from the rain and sun and can stand alone or be part of a deck.

Glossary

Grade: The finished level of the ground surrounding a landscaping or construction project. Also, the planned level of the ground around a project that is in progress.

Ground Fault Circuit Interrupter (GFCI): A device that monitors the loss of current in an electrical circuit. If an interruption occurs, the GFCI quickly shuts off current to that circuit. Codes require GFCIs on circuits near water, such as near a spa or ornamental pool.

Guardrail: An assembly of posts, balusters (or some other material), and rails that is installed around the edges of a deck for safety.

Handrail: A narrow railing at stairs that is designed to be grasped by the hand for support when ascending or descending.

Header joist: A building component that's attached to common joists, usually at a right angle, to help hold them in position and to provide rigidity.

Heartwood: The older, nonliving central wood of a tree, Usually darker and denser than younger outer layers of the tree (sapwood), heartwood sometimes has decay- and insect-resistant properties.

High-density polyethylene (HDPE): A petroleum-based dense plastic, often recycled from milk jugs and plastic bags, used to make composite lumber.

Ipe: A dense hardwood logged from tropical forests that is naturally resistant to rot, decay, insects, and fire.

Joist: A structural member, usually two-by lumber, commonly placed perpendicularly across beams to support deck boards.

Joist hanger: A metal framing connector used to join joists to a ledger board and header joists.

Lattice: An open framework made of wood, metal, or plastic strips—usually preassembled and typically in a crisscross pattern—that's used to build trellises, privacy and wind screens, and skirting to hide a deck's underside.

Ledger: An important structural component used to attach a deck to the side of a house.

Low-voltage lighting: Easy-to-install outdoor lighting fixtures that are powered by low-voltage direct current. (Transformers are used to convert 120-volt household current to 15 volts or less.)

Pergola: An ornamental, framed structure that is attached on one end to a wall and supported by posts or columns on the other. Pergolas are often used to provide shade on a deck.

Pier: A masonry support that rests on a footing and supports a beam. Pilaster: A decorative architectural detail that looks as though it's a rectangular column with a capital and base but in reality only projects slightly from an exterior wall.

Plan drawing: A drawing that shows an overhead view of the deck and specifies dimensions, along with the locations and sizes of components.

Post: A vertical member, usually 4x4 or 6x6, that supports a beam or railing.

Pressure-treated lumber: Wood that has had preservative forced into it under pressure to make it decay- and insect-resistant.

Proportion: The relationship of parts or objects to one another based on their size and commonly accepted rules of what looks pleasing to the eye.

PVC: A common thermoplastic resin, frequently called vinyl, used in a wide variety of building products.

Railing cap: A horizontal piece of lumber laid over the top rail that's often wide enough to set objects on. Railing caps sometimes cover post tops as well.

Riser: Vertical boards sometimes placed between stringers and under treads on stairs.

Scale: The relationship of a structure or building's size to people, nearby objects, and the surrounding space. Also, the relationship of elements of a structure to the whole.

Sealer: A water- or oil-based product applied to deck lumber to prevent moisture penetration and its damaging effects on wood. Also called water repellent.

Setback: The legally required distance of a structure or some other feature (a well or a septic system, for example) from the property line.

Site plan: A drawing that maps out a house and yard. Also called a base plan.

Skirt board: Solid band of horizontal wood members installed around the deck perimeter to conceal exposed ends of joists and deck boards.

Skirting: Material, generally made of narrow slats or lattice, that covers or screens the space between the edge of the deck and the ground.

Stringer: A wide, angled board that supports stair treads and risers.

Synthetic decking: Any engineered decking material made from plastics or composites.

Tongue and groove: A joint made by fitting a tongue on the edge of a board into a matching groove on the edge of another board.

Tread: The board you step on when using stairs.

Trellis: A structure designed to support vines that's used for ornamental purposes or to create privacy.

Ultraviolet (UV) light: The range of invisible radiation wavelengths, just beyond violet in the visible spectrum, that can be particularly damaging to outdoor wood structures such as decks.

Uplighting: A dramatic light treatment whereby a light is placed at the base of an object, pointing upward at it. This is an effective way to highlight trees, plantings, and architectural elements.

Vinyl: A shiny, tough, and flexible plastic that is used especially for flooring, siding, decking, and railing. Also called PVC.

Index

Index

Index

Photo Credits

page 1: Gary Rogers/Garden Collection **pages 3–7:** *all* Mark Lohman **page 8:** Liz Eddison/Garden Collection **page 10:** *both* Gary Rogers/Garden Collection **page 11:** Crandall & Crandall **page 12:** *top & bottom left* Roger Wade; *bottom right* Gary Rogers/Garden Collection **page 13:** Roger Wade **page 14:** *top* Michael S. Thompson; *bottom* Roger Wade **page 15:** *top* Liz Eddison/Garden Collection; *bottom* Roger Wade **page 16:** Nicola Stocken Tomkins/Garden Collection **page 17:** *top* Jonathon Buckley/Garden Collection; *bottom* Roger Wade **page 18:** *top left* Nicola Stocken Tomkins/Garden Collection; *top right* Liz Eddison/Garden Collection; *bottom* Gary Rogers/Garden Collection **page 19:** Jonathon Buckley/Garden Collection **page 20:** *top* courtesy of Dolphin Architects; *bottom* Jonathon Buckley/Garden Collection **page 21:** *top* Mark Lohman; *bottom* Liz Eddison/Garden Collection **page 22:** Marie O'Hara/Garden Collection **page 23:** *top* Roger Wade; *bottom* Ernest Braun, courtesy of California Redwood Association **page 24:** *top* Brian Vanden Brink, design: Horiuchi & Solien; *bottom* courtesy of Lloyd/Flanders Inc. **page 25:** *top* Rob Karosis; *bottom* courtesy of Shadetree **page 26:** *both* Roger Wade **page 27:** Robert Stubbert **page 28:** Roger Wade **page 29:** *top* Roger Wade; *bottom* Liz Eddison/Garden Collection **page 30-33:** *all* Mark Lohman **page 34:** *both* Roger Wade **page 35:** Mark Lohman **page 37:** Mark Lohman **page 36:** *top* Mark Lohman; *bottom* Rob Karosis **page 38:** Liz Eddison/Garden Collection **page 39:** *top* Liz Eddison/Garden Collection; *bottom* Roger Wade **page 40:** *top left & bottom* Derek St Romaine/Garden Collection; *top right* Jonathon Buckley/Garden Collection **page 41-42:** Mark Lohman **page 43:** *top* Roger Wade; *bottom* Gary Rogers/Garden Collection **page 44:** Liz Eddison/Garden Collection **page 45–47:** *all* Mark Lohman **page 48:** Jonathon Buckley/Garden Collection **page 49:** *top* Liz Eddison/Garden Collection; *bottom* Mark Lohman **page 50-55:** *all* Mark Lohman **pages 56-58:** both Mark Samu **page 59:** courtesy of Smart Deck **page 60:** *left* courtesy of Trex Decks; *right* Robert Perron, design: Robert Page **page 61:** *top* courtesy of Trex Decks; *bottom* courtesy of Cecco Trading, Inc. **pages 62–63:** *top right* courtesy of Summer Classics; *bottom right* Anne Gummerson; *bottom left* Mark Samu **page 64:**

courtesy of Western Cedar Lumber Association **page 65:** *top* Ernest Braun, courtesy of California Redwood Association, design: Scott Padgett; *bottom* Leslie Wright Dow, courtesy of California Redwood Association, design: Alex Porter **page 66:** courtesy of Trex Decks **page 67:** courtesy of Royal Crown Ltd. **page 68:** *top* courtesy of Royal Crown Ltd.; *bottom* courtesy of AridDeck **page 69:** courtesy of Cascades **page 70:** courtesy of Trex Decks **page 71:** top courtesy of Universal Forest Products; *bottom* courtesy of Sundance Spas **page 72:** *top* Robert Perron, design: Rai Muhlbauer; *bottom* courtesy of Summer Classics **page 73:** courtesy of CableRail by Feeney Architectural Products, design: Richard Shugar **page 74-79:** *all* Mark Lohman **page 80:** *top* Mark Lohman; *bottom* Beth Singer **page 81–98:** *all* Mark Lohman **page 99:** *top & center* Roger Wade; *bottom* Liz Eddison/Garden Collection **page 100–103:** *all* Mark Lohman **page 104:** *top left & right* Mark Lohman; *bottom left* Jonathon Buckley/Garden Collection; *bottom right* Liz Eddison/Garden Collection **page 105:** *top* Mark Lohman; *bottom left* Liz Eddison/Garden Collection; *bottom right* Nicola Stocken Tomkins/Garden Collection **page 106–113:** *all* Mark Lohman **page 114–115:** *all* Liz Eddison/Garden Collection **page 116:** Mark Lohman **page 117:** *top* Stan Sudol; *bottom* Liz Eddison/Garden Collection **page 118:** Beth Singer **page 119:** courtesy Hearth & Home **page 120:** *top left* Roger Wade; *top right & bottom* Liz Eddison/Garden Collection **page 121:** Mark Lohman **page 122–125:** *all* Gary Rogers/Garden Collection **page 126:** Derek Harris/Garden Collection **page 127:** *top* Liz Eddison/Garden Collection; *bottom* Torie Chugg/Garden Collection **page 128:** *top* courtesy of SunBriteTV; *bottom* courtesy of TIC Corporation **page 129:** courtesy of SunBriteTV **page 130:** *top* Liz Eddison/Garden Collection; *bottom* Andrew Lawson/Garden Collection **page 131:** Liz Eddison/Garden Collection **page 132:** *top* Gary Rogers/Garden Collection; *bottom* Liz Eddison/Garden Collection **page 133–136:** *all* Liz Eddison/Garden Collection **page 137:** Marie O'Hara/Garden Collection **page 138–140:** *all* Mark Lohman **page 141:** *top* Mark Lohman; *bottom* Liz Eddison/Garden Collection **page 142:** Nicola Stocken Tomkins/Garden Collection **page 143:**

Andrew Lawson/Garden Collection **page 144:** *top* Liz Eddison/Garden Collection; *bottom* Marie O'Hara/Garden Collection **page 145:** Liz Eddison/Garden Collection **page 146:** Jonathon Buckley/Garden Collection **page 147:** Andrew Lawson/Garden Collection **page 148–149:** *all* Liz Eddison/Garden Collection **page 150–154:** *all* Mark Lohman **page 155:** *top* Torie Chugg/Garden Collection; *bottom* Jerry Harpur/R.Davis Adams **page 156–159:** *all* Mark Lohman **page 160:** Gary Rogers/Garden Collection **page 161:** Torie Chugg/Garden Collection **page 162:** Jerry Harpur/Larry & Stephanie Feeny **page 163:** *top* Brad Simmons; *bottom* Brad Simmons/Greg Staley/Barry Wehrman/Cindy Martin **page 164:** *top* Liz Eddison/Garden Collection; *bottom* Marie O'Hara/Garden Collection **page 165:** Mark Lohman **page 166:** *top* Liz Eddison/Garden Collection; *bottom* Mark Lohman **page 167:** Roger Wade **page 168:** Mark Lohman **page 169:** *top left & bottom* Mark Lohman; *top right* Liz Nicola Stockton Tomkins/Garden Collection **page 170:** Jonathon Buckley/Garden Collection **page 171:** Julian Wass **page 172–173:** *all* Mark Lohman **page 174:** Liz Eddison/Garden Collection **page 176:** Derek St Romaine/Garden Collection **page 177:** *top* Liz Eddison/Garden Collection; *bottom* Derek St. Romaine/Garden Collection **page 178–180:** Liz Eddison/Garden Collection **page 181:** *top* Liz Marie O'Hara/Garden Collection; *bottom* Liz Eddison/Garden Collection **page 182–189:** *all* Liz Eddison/Garden Collection **page 190:** *top left* Jonathon Buckley/Garden Collection; *top right & bottom* Torie Chugg/Garden Collection **page 191:** Nicola Stockton Tomkins/Garden Collection **page 192–194:** *all* Liz Eddison/Garden Collection **page 196:** Derek St. Romaine/Garden Collection **page 197–198:** *all* Liz Eddison/Garden Collection **page 199:** Nicola Stockton Tomkins/Garden Collection **page 200:** *top* Nicola Stockton Tomkins/Garden Collection; *bottom* Derek Harris/Garden Collection **page 201:** Torie Chugg/Garden Collection **page 202:** *top* Nicola Stockton Tomkins/Garden Collection; *bottom* Derek Harris/Garden Collection **page 203:** *top* Liz Eddison/Garden Collection; *bottom* Gary Rogers/Garden Collection

If you like
Design Ideas for Decks and Patios,
take a look at these other books in the
Design Idea series

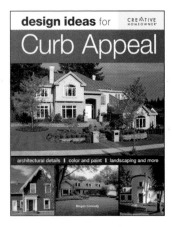
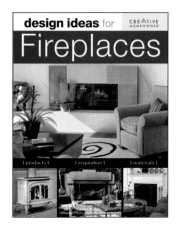

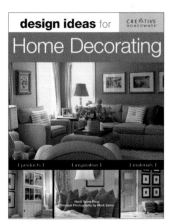